The Emergence of a Mexican Church

The Associate Reformed Presbyterian Church of Mexico

The cover design depicts the emerging Associate Reformed Presbyterian Church of Mexico in its growth from a small dependent denomination toward a strong autonomous Church of the future. Art work by George E. Mitchell.

THE EMERGENCE OF A MEXICAN CHURCH

The Associate Reformed Presbyterian Church of Mexico

James E. _Erskine_ Mitchell

William Carey Library

South Pasadena, California

International Standard Book Number: 0-87808-303-0
Library of Congress Catalog Number: 74-129189

Published by the William Carey Library
533 Hermosa Street
South Pasadena, Calif. 91030
Telephone 213-682-2047

PRINTED IN THE UNITED STATES OF AMERICA

To My Family,

Especially My Wife

Without Whose Help This Book

Would Have Never Been Written

CONTENTS

FIGURES

FOREWORD

Mr. and Mrs. James E. Mitchell have served as missionaries in Mexico under the Board of Foreign Missions of the Associate Reformed Presbyterian Church. Mr. Mitchell was appointed in 1961. Mrs. Mitchell went out after their marriage in 1963. Both of them have proved to be very active and useful workers. Mr. Mitchell served as business manager of the Neill E. Pressly Clinic in Ciudad Mante for the whole term.

The thesis here presented is the result of Mr. Mitchell's studies in the School of World Mission and Institute of Church Growth, Fuller Seminary, Pasadena, California. This is commended for the study of those interested in mission work, and especially in the Associate Reformed Presbyterian work in Mexico.

E. GETTYS, Secretary
Board of Foreign Missions

PREFACE

The Emergence of a Mexican Church is a case study of the growth of the Associate Reformed Presbyterian Church in Mexico. The author analyzes the historical facts - both negative and positive - and gives his interpretation of these, whether positive or negative, in the light of seven and one half years of experience on the field.

This study includes all the major aspects of the ninety years (1879-1969) during which the A. R. Presbyterian Church has had missionaries in Mexico, but it is primarily a preliminary study: hopefully it will arouse interest in our work and cause other missionaries, students of theology and churchmen to do further research on many of the items presented.

A preliminary outline of my plan of research was sent to forty key people of our denomination in the United States and Mexico. I asked for suggestions of any kind including matters not covered in the thesis. There were twenty- nine answers to this plea for help.

The task of writing involved many hours of archival and library research. The research library of the University of California at Los Angeles has the most extensive holdings. The Government Records Library at U.C.L.A. was also used. There I found official documents printed by the Mexican Government. The Fuller Theological Seminary Library was a rich source for general books on Mexico, church growth books and articles from other missionary literature.

The primary sources for the Associate Reformed Presbyterian Church data were books written by missionaries (past and

present) and the official Centennial and Sesquicentennial his-
tories printed by the order of Synod.

The Erskine College Library in Due West, South Carolina was
an essential source. Here the entire set of the *Minutes of the*
General Synod of the Associate Reformed Presbyterian Church are
preserved in a vault and are easily accessible. During the
early years of mission work in Mexico the annual reports of
each individual missionary were included in the *Minutes* and
these proved to be invaluable.

As I recorded the data obtained, definite positive and negative trends in church growth became evident. The positive aspects should be developed to their fullest extent and correct
procedures should be substituted for the negative facets.

With the help of the church growth principles learned during
this year (1969-1970) in the School of World Mission and Institute of Church Growth at Fuller Theological Seminary, some of
the answers will be attempted. But everyone who reads this
case study should be thinking of better ways to propagate the
Gospel so that many will be saved and take an active part in
the Church. It is hoped that these observations will be taken
as helpful tools, and not as direct criticism to any missionary
or the standard way of doing things.

All data was checked and compared for errors. Although most
of the material was taken from primary sources, secondary
sources were considered and used where relevant. The information was plotted on a graph in order to see the periods of
growth and non-growth. The graph is the basic tool in the
study. The figures used are field totals. For a more detailed
study each individual congregation should be analyzed.

The anthropological system of reference is used. It consists of the author's surname, the year and the page numbers
in parentheses within the text.

                                                    JAMES E. MITCHELL

ACKNOWLEDGMENTS

My sincere gratitude goes to all the professors of the School of World Mission and Institute of Church Growth at Fuller Theological Seminary, Pasadena, California. All of these men - Dr. Donald A. McGavran, Dr. Alan R. Tippett, Dr. Charles H. Kraft, Mr. C. Peter Wagner and Mr. Roy E. Shearer - have given me many hours of their time and concern, but special thanks go to my advisor, Dr. Ralph D. Winter.

I express my deep appreciation to those who answered my letter asking for suggestions for the preliminary outline. They are:

L. M. Allison	Kathryn Galloway	Mary Alice Mitchell
G. F. Archer	W. C. Halliday	W. F. Mitchell
Margaret Blakely	John Kimmons	G. E. Morrison
Milton Blakely	Nancy Kimmons	Grady Oates
R. L. Brawley	W. C. Lauderdale	Betty Sides
R. L. Brunson	Mabel McGill	David Sides
Ruben Castaneda	John McGill	J. T. Stephenson
P. G. Covone	David Michaelis	J. Rogers White
Florence Craig	Vicky Michaelis	R. A. Whitesides
Janus DeHamer	C. L. Mitchell	

Grateful appreciation is also extended to Dr. W. W. Boyce and Dr. E. Gettys for the time given in personal interviews. Thanks go to those who took time to write letters to the author so that this study could be done with accuracy.

R. L. Brawley   Ascencion Juarez
R. L. Brunson   Maurilio Lopez L.
Ruben Castaneda   Amador Pesina Gonzalez
P. G. Covone   Harriett Lou Whitesides
Flora Harper Halliday Robert A. Whitesides
W. C. Halliday

I appreciate the tedious editing done by Mrs. Ralph D. Winter and the many hours spent by my wife making corrections and typing the drafts. The lettering was done by Mrs. Roy E. Shearer. My nephew, George E. Mitchell, did the art work on the cover.

INTRODUCTION

This study of the growth of the Associate Reformed Presbyterian Church in Mexico gives an objective evaluation of the
ninety years of the mission endeavor of the sister Church in
the U. S. A.   During the first years, it chiefly deals with
the foreign missionaries who pioneered in the work there.   In
later years we see that the Mexicans are taking more and more
of the responsibilities upon themselves.   This brings us to
the contemporary dilemma.   How can we have a truly indigenous
Church by the centennial year, 1979?   Can the transition be
made in ten years that has not been achieved in nine decades?

Mexico is on the move.   She is perhaps the most stable
country in Latin America.   Yet there are many changes taking
place.   More people are in schools than ever before; many of
the poor have socialized medicine; large groups are moving from
rural areas to large urban centers; and Protestants can witness freely without being harassed.   It is now time for action.
With God's help the impossible becomes reality.   God can use
weak people to do great things.   If His people (missionary
and national; lay and ordained) make themselves available, we
can see a dream come true.   We will not only have an autonomous
Church, but a growing fellowship extending throughout Mexico
and into other parts of the world.

1

Historical Background of
Mexico and Our Mission

THE BIBLICAL BASIS FOR MISSIONS

Why should a Church send missionaries to a foreign field?
Is there not work to do in our own country? Is it God's will
that we send out missionaries to other lands?

> Christian mission exists for the purpose of bringing men
> to Christ and forming fellowships or congregations into
> which they are incorporated as local groups of the great
> Church Universal (Tippett 1969: 155).

This concept of the church's mission indicates action. It is
not simply a statement of doctrine, but rather an action where
the Gospel is proclaimed and new churches are formed.

God's Command

The scriptural basis for missions can be found in both the
Old and New Testaments. The book of beginnings records God's
promise to Abram in Genesis 12:3 (R. S. V.):

> I will bless those who bless you, and him who curses you
> I will curse; and by you all the families of the earth
> shall bless themselves.

We read in Isaiah 49:6 (R. S. V.):

> He says: It is too light a thing that you should be my
> servant to raise up the tribes of Jacob and to restore
> the preserved of Israel; I will give you as a light to

the nations, that my salvation may reach to the end of
the earth.

We see a direct command of Jesus Christ to His disciples regarding this in Matthew 28:19-20 (R. S. V.):

> Go therefore and make disciples of all nations, baptizing
> them in the name of the Father and of the Son and of the
> Holy Spirit, teaching them to observe all that I have
> commanded you; and lo, I am with you always to the close
> of the age.

The same idea is recorded in Acts 1:8 (R. S. V.):

> But you shall receive power when the Holy Spirit has
> come upon you; and you shall be my witnesses in Jerusalem
> and in all Judea and Samaria and to the end of the earth.

Christ, the Head of the Church, says that we, the body of
His Church must go and be His witnesses in Jerusalem (our own
home or town), in Judea (our homeland), in Samaria (our foreign
neighbor, like Mexico) and to the ends of the earth (other
nations around the world such as Pakistan, Japan, Africa, etc.).
The Associate Reformed Presbyterian Church, accepting and re-
sponding to these imperatives, has missionaries in the United
States, in Mexico and in West Pakistan.

There are many other passages from the Word of God to sub-
stantiate the mission enterprise. Paul was called to proclaim
the good news of Jesus Christ in a land that was not his homeland. Acts 16:9 (R. S. V.) says:

> And a vision appeared to Paul in the night: a man of
> Macedonia was standing beseeching him and saying, 'Come
> over to Macedonia and help us.'

Although Macedonia was a colony of the Roman Empire and Paul
as a Roman citizen probably did not experience as much cultural change as most missionaries do today, this was a foreign
mission for the apostle. He responded to the call immediately
going to Phillipi, the leading city of Macedonia, to begin his
mission work. Paul recognized, however, with a deep convic-
tion that the gospel message should be proclaimed to all. We
read in Romans 1:14-15 (R. S. V.):

> I am under obligation both to Greeks and to barbarians,
> both to the wise and to the foolish: so I am eager to
> preach the gospel to you also who are in Rome.

We too, with the same urgency as Paul, should preach the Gospel to every creature in response to the love we have received from God and in obedience to His command to the redeemed. I John 4:21b (R. S. V.) declares: "that he who loves God should love his brother also." We have been saved by grace through faith freely offered by God in Jesus Christ. In John 3:16 (R. S. V.) comes the message of the Gospel:

> For God so loved the world that he gave his only Son, that whoever believes in him should not perish but have eternal life.

We love God because He loved us first and therefore, we must love our neighbor also. We should desire for our neighbor the same blessing of salvation that we have experienced.

In sending missionaries to Mexico and Pakistan, the Associate Reformed Presbyterian Church is striving actively to obey God's command to go and disciple the nations. This imperative to go, however, must be rightly understood to include the extension of the Church in the homeland as well as the extension of the Kingdom of God in other lands. The divine commission includes the secular world at our own door along with the masses throughout the world. Therefore each Christian should be a witness, dedicated to the proclamation of the Gospel. This proclamation which in turn becomes church extension, begins at the local level. Then by the leading and guidance of the Holy Spirit, the Church extends to other communities and even to the end of the world. This ministry is the privilege and responsibility of all those within the fellowship of the Church.

The Associate Reformed Presbyterian Response

Realizing this, the A. R. P. Church first formally expressed its interest in the cause of world missions in 1837 with the formation of a Board of Foreign Missions. It was not until 1878, however, that the Board began to consider Mexico as a mission field. After beginning missionary efforts in Liberia, Africa in 1845 which were unsuccessful and after deciding to join in a cooperative effort with the United Presbyterian Church in Egypt, the fires of missionary zeal burst into flame and the Synod took the following action in session in 1878:

> Resolved 1st: That Synod hereby renews its pledge to sustain our first Missionary, Mrs. M. E. Giffen, in Egypt.
> 2nd. That the Synod will enlarge its Foreign Missionary Work.

3rd. That in said enlargement we will establish an independent Mission.
4th. That said independent Mission be established in
Mexico.
5th. That the Board of Foreign Missions be directed to
select the field and make all necessary arrangements to
send out a Missionary as soon as practicable (Galloway
1905:6-7).

Thus we, the A. R. P. Church, sent out our first missionaries under our own Board to Mexico in 1879.

THE MEXICAN CULTURE

Background

Mexico has a great heritage. Even before the Spanish
arrived she had had two advanced civilizations. The first was
that of the Maya Indians which lasted from about the third
century B. C. to the thirteenth century. It prevailed throughout part of Central America, the Pennisula of Yucatan, Tabasco,
Chiapas and a great part of Oaxaca and Vera Cruz. The second
was the Nahuatl culture which had its center in the mysterious
lost city of Tolan. The Nahuatl family included the Toltecs,
skilled artisans who built the now famous pyramids and temples
of Teotihuacan. One tribe of the Nahuatl family, the Aztecs,
established itself in the valley of Mexico and founded the
present Mexico City, the capital of the country.

The Maya civilization had priests as their governing class.
These priests were mainly occupied with ritual and the study
of arts and sciences. In an artistic sense they excelled and
their astronomical calculations were surprisingly exact. However, their religion has been described as barbarous. Human
sacrifice was practiced and children, particularly orphans,
were often chosen as the victims. The following testimony by
a young Maya vividly portrays the ritual.

> The priests handed over the candles they held, and four
> of them caught hold of the boy and placed him in a supine
> position, holding him by his hands and feet. Pedro Euan,
> taking the flint knife, made an opening on the left side
> of the youth's heart, grasped the heart and cut the arte-
> ries with his knife. He gave the severed heart to the
> priest, Gaspar Chim, who made two cuts like a cross in
> its extremity and then raised it on high. Next he took
> some part ... and placed it in the mouth of the largest
> of the idols (Thompson 1966:281).

The common people were treated as beasts of burden and were a prey to folk beliefs, fanaticism and oppresive slavery. Remnants of this way of life are still noticeable in present day Mexico. Although the Mayas almost certainly practiced human sacrifice in all periods of their history, it was never on the same scale as by the Aztecs.

The Aztecs were notable as a powerful and warlike people. They traded extensively, were quite aggresive in their conquests and depended economically on horticulture. Spirits, gods and ghosts were prevalent in their world. There was no one supreme god, but four of their deities were more important than the rest. The first, Tezcatlipoca, had a dual character of both good and evil. The second, Quetzalcoatl, was the divinity of wind and air, the special patron of the priesthood. He supposedly had disappeared and was expected to return as a Messiah. Huitzilopochtli, the third, was the god of war and therefore especially important. And fourth was Thalocs, a group of divinities in control of rain, thunder and the mountains. Along with these were many separate gods, all having their special cults, priests and ceremonies.

The performance of sacrifice was the chief function of the priests. Human offerings were used. How many lives were annually sacrificed can only be estimated. Cortes reportedly found a temple at Mexico City with 160,000 skulls in it. A historian has described the custom like this.

> The victim was laid on his back. Two priests held his arms, two his legs and one his head. Then another priest with a sharp stone instrument, with a quick skillful thrust, opened the breast and with one hand tore out the still palpitating heart and offered it to the sun ... After this, the body was thrown headlong down the steps where it was taken by the owner, cut into pieces and distributed to be cooked and eaten. Before being cut up, the body was flayed and young men put on the skins and disported themselves in mock warfare (Braden 1930:56).

This was the situation when in 1521 Hernando Cortes and his small army of about six hundred Spainards arrived at the coast of Mexico. There were approximately six million Indians in the country at the time of the Spanish Conquest. Nevertheless, Cortes and his handful of men met little opposition. Since Cortes burned his ships after landing, the men knew they could not retreat. They must conquer or die. And so after a siege lasting almost three months the Aztec capital fell to the Spainards.

Several factors favored Cortes' success. While at the island of Cozumel before landing on the mainland, a Spainard who
had been a captive of the Indians managed to escape and reach
the ships. He became invaluable to Cortes as an interpreter as
he had lived among the Indians long enough to acquire the language. Dona Marina, an Indian woman, was given to the invader
as a mistress and she aided him as a guide and also as an interpreter. One other unique circumstance entered into the picture. Quetzacoatl, an Aztec god, had departed with the promise
that one day he would return out of the east with bearded,
white people who should rule Mexico. He had prophesied that he
would return in a certain year in the cycle of fifty-two years
which made up the Mexican calendar. Hernando Cortes landed on
Mexican soil on that year and the Indians were convinced that
their "messiah" had returned. They soon discovered their mis-
take, but it was too late. The Spanish had conquered Mexico
and thus began a period of slavery, killings and general mistreatment of the Indians by the Spanish.

Cortes has been described as "greedy, debauched, a politi-
cian without scruples" (Ricard 1966:15). Admittedly he was
attracted by the gold in Mexico yet the conquest also carried
a spiritual imperative as seen in the instructions given Cortes
by Don Diego de Velazquez, the governor of Cuba known then as
the Spanish Island, under whose orders the expedition had taken
place.

> You must bear in mind from the beginning that the first
> aim of your expedition is to serve God and spread the
> Christian Faith ... Finally you must neglect no oppor-
> tunity to spread the knowledge of the True Faith and the
> Church of God among those people who dwell in darkness
> (Ricard 1966:16).

Yet despite the many good intentions the enterprise has been
termed by many as chiefly imperialistic. As was typical of
their time the Spanish *conquistadores* had little respect for
human life. They ruled the country with an iron hand, killed
many people and seized large amounts of gold and silver which
they sent to Spain. In addition they did many other grotesque
things. This unhealthy situation lasted for three hundred
years. The presence of the foreigners contributed to an up-
surge of a *mestizo* population, persons of mixed European and
Indian blood. Thousands of Indians became nothing more than
slaves, many drifting hopelessly in a civilization which
offered them nothing materially nor spiritually.

Religion and Politics

There was strong connection between religion and politics.

With the   Spanish conquerors came the Roman Catholic religion.
Missionaries accompanied and followed the *conquistadores*. The
Franciscans were the first priests to arrive, later to be
joined by the Dominicans, the Augustinians and the Jesuits.
Their primary objective was to baptize and catechize the Indi-
ans. Cortes ordered all the Indian idols destroyed and buried.
Such a transformation from pagan idolatry to a form of Roman
Catholocism was not easy and it met with great resistance. How-
ever, once more the conquerors prevailed and the idols were
torn down.

> And so the cross of Christ was planted in Mexico. Tragi-
> cally it was not on Him but on an image of the Virgin
> Mary that ... worship was centered. Tragically, too,
> these first hastily baptized adherents learned only the
> form, not the spirit of worship (McClelland 1960:5).

There are factors that favored and those that hindered the
work of the Roman Catholic missionaries.

Factors Favoring Conversion of the Indians
1. The similarities, real or apparent, between the two
   forms of religion.
2. The high character of the early missionaries.
3. The support and cooperation of the government, both
   imperial and local.
4. The character of the Indians.

Factors Hindering Conversion of the Indians
1. The hostile or indifferent attitude of the Spanish toward the conversion of the Indians.
2. The evil examples set by the Spainards.
3. The gross mistreatment of the Indians.
4. The lower moral character of the priests who came
   later.
5. The conflict between the religious orders and even
   more that between the secular and regular clergy
   (Braden 1930:180).

The priests had four methods of christianizing the Indians:
teaching, preaching, suppression of idolatry and the general
use of authority. [This plan met with almost unbelievable
success in the first fifty years of mission endeavor as we see
that churches were constructed, institutions were founded and
the entire populace of the great central plateau was declared
Christian at the end of that period.]

The priests, however, took undue advantage of their authority. The Indians, accustomed to docility under their former
rulers, were willing to follow the desires of their masters

and be baptized. They soon learned that a professed conversion was protection from further Spanish cruelty. In great
masses they went to the priests asking for baptism. As a result the rite was performed indiscriminately with little or no
preparation or instruction.

> I and the brother who was with me baptized in this pro-
> vince of Mexico upwards of 200,000 persons - so many in
> fact that I cannot give an accurate estimate of the num-
> ber. Often we baptized in a single day 14,000 people,
> sometimes 10,000, sometimes 8,000 (Neill 1964:169).

The missionaries under influence of the European custom
where baptism was administered to masses of infants found it
easy to baptize the Indians in great numbers because they believed them to be an ignorant people, incapable of much instruction. In defense of their actions they asked: "Could the
gates of the Kingdom of God be closed to these simple souls,
full of good will?" (Ricard 1966:85). This mass Christianiza-
tion without evangelical conversion extended the European
pattern of a nominal Church with little spirituality, a condition that is still prevalent today.

The first priests lived good lives, adopted a standard of
living just like the Indians and worked hard to do the proper
things with and for them, but this situation soon deteriorated.
Soon the friars began to forget their mission, thinking instead of wealth and position.

Social stratification developed with the higher clergy and
European born Spainards at the top holding all the religious,
political, social and economic power in their hands. Next were
the creoles, Mexican born Spainards, who although fairly
wealthy had little power and were ineligible for positions of
authority in the Church, state and army. Next were the *mestizos*, usually without land or rights; and lastly, the Indians. It was the example of the American Revolution plus dis-
satisfaction with this situation that fostered a revolt led by
a village priest, Don Miguel Hidalgo. Devoted to the welfare
of his people and dedicated to obtaining human rights for the
great masses, Hidalgo gave the call for revolt on September
16, 1810. Although failing in its primary objective, the revolt did lead to the complete independence of Mexico from
Spain in 1821.

The Roman Catholic Church continued to dominate the political, educational and religious life. The clergy owned at
least half of all the land and controlled most of the wealth.
Yet in spite of the wealth of the Church, most of her adherents

were living in degradation. Only children of the aristocrats
were received in the church supported schools. The Bible was
an unknown book. The priesthood had greatly degenerated with
the exception of a few whose character and devotion remained
unbesmirched.

The first fifty years of independence were chaotic. The
situation was complicated by the North American invasion in
1847 in which Mexico lost more than half her territory. The
second half of the nineteenth century was marked by the tri-
umph of the Liberal Party under the inspiration of Benito
Juarez. A pure-blood Indian who has been called the Abraham
Lincoln of Mexico after the man whom he most admired, Juarez
led his party in the formulation of the Constitution of 1857
and the famous Laws of Reform. His wise statement: *"El
respeto al derecho ajeno es la paz"* appears on his statue in
the *plazas* of many Mexican towns. One must agree with Juarez
that respect for the rights of others is the basis of peace.

Economics

The Constitution of 1857 and the Laws of Reform provided
for freedom of religion, separation of Church and State, the
nationalization of the property of the clergy, lay teaching
in the official schools and civil marriage. These reform
laws were really the first steps toward a solid foundation of
Mexican government. Although the laws seemed to be aimed
against the Roman Catholic faith, they were in reality against
the Roman hierarchy.

During the period of the fifties there were several civil
wars which finally broadened into the international arena
when Great Britain, Spain and France jointly invaded Mexico,
supposedly to collect debts. The first two withdrew when
they realized that Napoleon III had staged the invasion to gain
political control of Mexico. Juarez and his Republican government were run out of the capital and Napoleon placed Maximilian
of Hapsburg on the throne as emperor. He was supported by
the conservative elements of the country. Maximilian, however,
was a disappointment to all. He did not govern well and then
unwisely split with the French. Napoleon, under diplomatic
and domestic pressure, withdrew the French troops and the Republican armies surged back into Mexico City. Maximilian was
captured and shot thus closing another phase of Mexican history.

In 1876 with the death of Juarez, Porfirio Diaz became
president of Mexico and was actually dictator of the country
until 1911 with the exception of one four year period from
1880-1884. He encouraged foreign investment and made it easy

for people from other parts of the world to immigrate into
Mexico. This opened the doors for our first missionaries to
enter *Los Estados Unidos Mexicanos* in 1879. Although the
reign of Diaz was in some respects good for the country in an
economic sense, many of the people were just as poor as before. Transportation, industry and commerce developed rapidly
and Mexico for the first time gained a place of pride and respect among the nations. But the masses only went deeper into
debt to the few rich landowners. Those who had money made
more and those who had little became poorer. Discontent was
seething beneath the appearance of prosperity.

A CHURCH IS PLANTED

The Setting

To such a Mexico went Neill Erskine Pressly, son of an
A. R. Presbyterian minister. He and his wife were the first
missionaries of our Board. Arriving in Mexico City on January 14, 1879, the Presslys fulfilled the resolution taken by
our Synod the preceding year to establish an independent
mission in Mexico. They spent almost a year studying the
language and looking over the field. Then by arrangement with
other denominations already working in Mexico, and with the
consent of their own Board, they located in Tampico, the state
of Tamaulipas.

The Mexico which these pioneer missionaries would at least
in part be seeking to claim for Jesus Christ in the name of
the A. R. P. Church, by 1879 following immense annexation by
the U. S. which reduced Mexico to half its former area, still
covered 761,600 square miles, making it approximately one-
fourth the size of the new expanded United States mainland.
On the north it has a 1,614 mile border with the United States.
On the south it borders British Honduras and Guatemala. There
are some 5,728 miles of coastline on the east with the Carib-
bean Sea and the Gulf of Mexico and on the west with the Pacific Ocean. Mexico is made up mainly of a great central plateau which reaches an elevation of 18,209 feet above sea level
at its highest point in the Peak of Orizaba. The Sierra Madre
Occidental, a long mountain range, forms the western rim of
the plateau. For hundreds of years it was a natural barrier
to transportation between the plateau and the west coast.
Paved roads and a railroad system were built across it in the
early 1900's. This plateau is also bound on the east by a
similar mountain range, the Sierra Madre Oriental. In addition
to the extensive plateau, there are five other land areas in
Mexico: the Pacific Northwest, the Southern Uplands, the

Chiapas Highlands, the Yucatan Pennisula and the Gulf Coastal
Plain. It was in this latter that the Presslys located.

The state of Tamaulipas borders with the United States and
has 250 miles of coastline along the Gulf of Mexico from
Brownsville, Texas to Tampico which is situated in the southern-
most tip. The Tropic of Cancer runs through the state thus
explaining why it is known as the *tierra caliente*, the hot
country. The summer temperatures are high with the only cool
months being December and January. Agriculture abounds because of the eternal summer.

Tampico, though not the state capital, was and still is one
of the principal cities. Located at the juncture of the Panuco and Tamesi Rivers, six miles up from the Gulf coast, it had
a population of approximately 17,000 at the time the Presslys
arrived. Because of its location Tampico gained importance
as a seaport, ranking second only to Vera Cruz. At the time
Mr. Pressly began work there, the Standard Oil Company had a
large operation in the surrounding area. See accompanying map
and chart for pertinent information concerning the geography
and the population of Mexico.

The Religious Climate

The first Protestants who entered Mexico were chaplains
accompanying the United States troops in the encounter in 1846.
With the acceptance of the Constitution of 1857 came a soften-
ing of the position of the government concerning evangelicals
and so even that early a few missionaries began entering the
country locating in Matamoros, Monterrey and Mexico City. The
religious climate they found was of course that presented by
the Roman Catholic Church with the virgin Mary being the central figure. A Catholic historian has written:

> Important in the conversion of the Indians was the de-
> votion to our Lady of Guadalupe, which spread through-
> out the land and by the 17th century was the charac-
> teristic devotion of the Mexican people (Olmedo 1967:771).

Others have affirmed that devotion to the Virgin is more important in Mexico than the worshipping of Christ. The Church
had presented Christ as a defeated, dying victim, a man on a
cross, a man of sorrows.

> In most Mexican crucifixes our Redeemer appears so
> bloody that one gets the impression that the sculptor
> ... enjoyed depicting blood, and sometimes the blood

PLATE 1

LAND REGIONS OF MEXICO:
TOTAL AREA IN COMPARISON WITH UNITED STATES

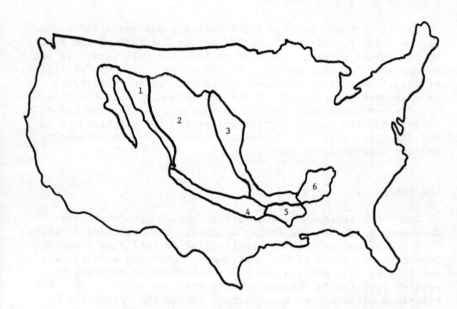

1. The Pacific Northwest

2. The Plateau of Mexico

3. The Gulf Coastal Plain

4. The Southern Uplands

5. The Chiapas Highlands

6. The Yucatan Peninsula

Source: Aschmann, Brandenburg, Brothers and Quirk 1970:375

PLATE 2

POPULATION STATISTICS OF MEXICO 1875-1970
COMPARISON OF SOCIAL STATISTICS

YEAR	TOTAL POP.	EUROPEAN	MESTIZO	INDIGENES	PER CENT LITERACY	PER CENT RURAL	PER CENT URBAN	UPPER CLASS	MIDDLE CLASS	LOWER CLASS
1875	9,495,000	1,899,000	4,083,000	3,513,000	9					
1880	10,448,000	1,985,000	4,493,000	3,970,000	10					
1895	12,632,000	2,526,000	5,306,000	4,800,000	14	81	19	1.44%	7.78%	90.78%
1900	13,607,000	2,700,000	5,886,000	5,021,000	18	80	20			
1910	15,160,000	2,729,000	7,822,000	5,609,000	20	77.7	22.3			
1921	14,334,000		10,224,000	4,110,000	34	74.7	25.3			
1930	16,553,000		13,965,000	2,648,000	39	66	34			
1940	19,654,000		16,607,000	2,945,000	48	65	35	1.05%	15.87%	83.08%
1950	25,891,000		23,502,000	2,889,000	56	57	43			
1960	34,923,000		31,291,000	3,632,000	62	49	51			
1965	42,000,000		34,500,000	7,500,000	78	45	55			
1970	50,000,000		40,000,000	10,000,000	90	40	60	3%	17%	80%

Note: 1965 and 1970 data are estimates.

Sources: Cumberland 1968:367
         Cline 1962a:382

drops really look like rubies ... and one wonders whether,
in this country, he was not unconsciously equated with
the victim of an Aztec human sacrifice (Considine 1966:
44).

In contrast, Mary became a symbol of beauty always accessible
and benevolent. She became known as the mediatrix between
the worshipper and God, the giver of life, the source of
health and the means of power.

The veneration of the virgin Mary was begun with the initial
evangelistic thrust of the Roman Catholics, but the special
emphasis on Our Lady of Guadalupe who was to become the patron
saint of Mexico has its own story. On December 9, 1531, the
Indian Juan Diego, a man more than fifty years old and just
recently converted reported that he saw the Virgin Mary at
Tepeyac, a hill northwest of Mexico City. She instructed
him to have the bishop build a church on that site. Three
days later Juan saw a second apparition. This time the Virgin
told him to pick some flowers and take them to the bishop. He
found some roses in a spot where only cactus had previously
grown and following directions picked them and carried them
to the bishop in his mantle. When he opened his mantle to
present the flowers to the bishop the roses fell out and beneath them was the painted image of the Lady. It is thus that
the "brown virgin" has been associated in the minds of thousands as a deity in her own right. The full extent of this
can be seen on December 12 on Guadalupe Day when the entire
country renders a fervent tribute to the virgin and as some
have described it, "paradoxically to the devil" (McClelland
1960:8).

The first sanctuary honoring Our Lady of Guadalupe was
erected in 1533. Later additions and new sanctuaries have
been built on the same site which is still today the mecca of
many thousands of Roman Catholics in Mexico. Interestingly,
historians tell us that the place where the Basilica of Guadalupe is located was once the location of a temple to a pagan
goddess.

> Nor was it true only in the case of the Virgin of Guada-
> lupe that the Christian sanctuary was erected on the spot
> where formerly there had been a pagan sanctuary. The
> same is true of the *Virgen de los Remedios,* of the *Senor
> del Sacromonte,* of the *Senor de Chalma,* and of many
> other centers of pilgrimage (Considine 1966:50).

Even the present massive Catholic Cathedral in Mexico City
stands on the site which was once the location of one of the
greatest pagan temples.

So it was that the first Protestant missionaries began to invade the country to carry the message of a living faith in our Lord and Saviour, Jesus Christ. Their highest purposes were not to proselytize nor to oppose the Roman Church, but simply to evangelize. The situation demanded the presence of these evangelicals as the heralds of the good news are known, because as one writer explained in his discussion on the growth and ministry of the Roman Catholic Church in Mexico:

> Thus the faith of the Mexicans, nominally Catholic, lacks the spirit, the uniformity, and solidarity that characterize the faith elsewhere ... Instead of conquering Mexico with an exclusive opportunity to do so for three centuries the Catholic church has been conquered by it (Gruening 1940:273).

Dr. and Mrs. Neill Erskine Pressly

Dr. and Mrs. N. E. Pressly encountered great opposition that had already developed toward the evangelical movement. Their own ministry was discouraging and the establishment of a Protestant mission in Tampico was exceedingly difficult. The Northern Presbyterian Church had already experienced problems in seeking to open mission work there earlier and thus had been quite willing and eager to abandon the field in favor of the Associate Reformed Presbyterians. Two of the main obstacles which thwarted the Presslys' efforts were an active anti-Protestant feeling and the work of the Spiritualists.

An old warehouse served as a chapel and for more than a year services were held regularly with only the missionary, his family and a Mexican minister in attendance. The native minister was the Rev. Pedro Trujillo. Born and educated in Mexico City, he had been saved through the preaching of a converted Catholic priest. He was at first connected with the Episcopal Church and then transferred his membership to the Presbyterian Church U. S. in which he took a Bible course having in view the work of an evangelist. This Church sent him to Tampico to open the field for the Gospel and he labored there until the area was transferred to our Mission and the Presslys arrived on the scene. By his own request he at that time joined with our efforts.

Finally after eighteen months of holding services the first ray of encouragement came with the baptism of a poor old blind woman, Jesus Gonzalez. Soon others took courage and accepted the Lord Jesus as their Saviour. In June, 1881, a congregation of fifteen members was organized. The Lord's

Supper was observed for the first time on July 3, 1881, with
fifteen communicants partaking.

HARD TIMES AT FIRST

Thus there were hard times at first. A letter from Dr.
Pressly to the Synod written in August of that same year gave
the state of the Mission and underlined the discouragements
and difficulties through which they were passing. Here are
portions selected from it.

> To the Board of Foreign Missions--Gentlemen: The end of
> another Synodical year approaches and your Missionary
> begs to present the following: The past year has had its
> sorrows, its discouragements, and its encouragements ...
> The health of Tampico has been remarkably good the entire
> year with Vera Cruz, most fatally scourged with Yellow
> fever. The heat has been very severe and as yet we have
> not had the customary rains. My assistant in the months
> of October and November of the past year was confined to
> his bed for six weeks, his attack being a form of brain
> fever. Regular service has been held three times a week
> in the chapel: twice on the Sabbath day and on Wednes-
> day night. The attendance varies from twenty to thirty
> odd. The great discouraging feature of the year is the
> indifference of the masses to everything spiritual. We
> did not have any of the fanatical spirit that seemed to
> prevail throughout the interior in the spring, but
> there is an opposition, a hatred among all the better
> classes to the Protestant cause, that influences in a
> greater or less degree those of the lower classes. The
> least ridicule will embitter them against the cause ...
> I desire to call the attention of the Board to the
> necessity of an appropriate house of worship. Property
> has almost doubled itself in the past six months. The
> growth of the place, the ideas of this people and the
> success of the work demand it ... If the work is to be
> permanent some such step should be taken. Humanly
> speaking, I think it would be a great stimulus.
>   I am, respectfully,   NEILL E. PRESSLY
> Tampico, Tam., August 29th, 1881 (Associate Reformed
> Presbyterian Church 1881:10-11).

In the ensuing years, notwithstanding fanaticism and in-
difference aggravated by political disturbances, the work progressed. In 1885, Neill E. Pressly was ordered by the Board
of Foreign Missions to organize a presbytery to be known as
the Presbytery of Tampico. This pioneer missionary in addition
to his labors in the city had explored the surrounding

countryside on horseback, going as far as one hundred miles
south of Tampico into the state of Vera Cruz and had been able
to preach the Gospel in five different stations. Because of
the territory covered and the difficulties of travel, he was
unable to carry out the instructions of his Board concerning
the organization of a presbytery at that time.

By 1887 the home Board and Synod thought the mission endeavor merited more help and so sent out to the field to join
the Presslys, the Rev. and Mrs. J. S. A. Hunter. That same
year one thousand copies of the *Psalter*, the A. R. P. song
book,were printed in Spanish with thirty-four different selec-
tions. Also one hundred copies of the *Book of Church Order*
translated by Dr. Pressly came off the press. It seemed that
the area was beginning to open up to the Gospel. Appeals
had come from three towns in Vera Cruz - Tantoyuca, Tuxpam and
Tantima - asking that someone be sent to them to preach the
good news of Jesus Christ.

However, the next year's report from the field sounded a
discouraging note, bearing the news that there was almost
universal sickness, that one of the native ministers, Rev.
Zenon Zaleta, had died and that the mission cause was at a
standstill. Mr. Zaleta was the first man to be won for Christ
by the A. R. P. Mission in Mexico. He was deeply moved by
the Christian truth and abandoned his blacksmith's trade to
study with Dr. Pressly in preparation for the ministry.
Granted a license to preach by his teacher in 1885 he was
noted as a sincere humble man with a burning desire to win
souls for Christ. Thus his death coming just three short years
later was a blow and was felt heavily by missionary and native
alike.

A Presbytery Organized in 1888

The one step of progress coming out of that dismal year was
the organization of the Presbytery of Tampico on June 29, 1888.
Dr. Pressly met in Tampico in the rented chapel with two Mexican ministers, Pedro Trujillo and Zenon Zaleta (his death came
two months later); Elder Pablo Morato; and the licentiates
Inez Hernandez and N. Arrebalo for the purpose of organizing
a presbytery. Dr. Pressly stated the object of the meeting,
preached a sermon based on Acts 18:9-11 (King James Version):

> Then spake the Lord to Paul in the night by a vision,
> Be not afraid, but speak, and hold not thy peace: For
> I am with thee, and no man shall set on thee to hurt
> thee: for I have much people in this city. And he
> continued there a year and six months, teaching the

word of God among them.

and then constituted the Presbytery of Tampico with prayer.
The above names plus that of Mr. Hunter newly arrived on the
field were placed on the roll. Inez Hernandez was ordained at
that first meeting. Mr. Hernandez came from an Indian village
in Vera Cruz. He had been reached by the Gospel through the
witness of Zenon Zaleta and Dr. Pressly. Coming from a poverty
stricken family with a gambler for a father this young man
dedicated his life to the ministry and after a short course of
study with Dr. Pressly, most of which was carried on by
correspondence, he was ordained.

The Work Growing Amid Hardships

The Hunters decided upon Ciudad del Maiz in the state of San
Luis Potosi as the center of their missionary operations. At
the time of their location there, the mountain town had some
six thousand inhabitants. Opposition was described as strong.

At the end of the first decade of A.R.P. involvement in
missionary activity in Mexico, preaching was being done in
twelve points with the base of operations still being in Tampico. Two hundred twenty-six members were reported. The next
years were full of hardships. The longed-for church building
was constructed in Tampico, yet attendance dropped. In Ciudad
del Maiz the missionaries were the victims of stone throwers.
When this persecution ceased, the tongues began to wag, severe-
ly criticizing any who dared enter the Protestant chapel services. This was even more damaging to the mission cause than
were the stones.

Perhaps nothing more succintly gives the state of the
Mission, the hardships through which they were passing and
the discouragement which they felt than a roll call of some
of the preaching stations: Tampico, the work not advancing
and the city in the midst of a great flu epidemic; Pueblo
Viego, not much hope - some have died; Tampico Alto, abandoned,
minister turned against Protestants; Panuco, holding its own,
but no minister available to serve there; Vega de Otates, potential growth, but no minister; Chiconcillo, area of great
growth now experiencing difficulties among people in regard
to land; Palo Blanco, work at a standstill; Tapa Boca, nothing
happening; El Estaco, work suspended, no worker; and Tantima,
prospects seem encouraging.

It was noted at this time that our Church was the only one
working in Mexico that had located a center on the coast and
that maintained foreign workers in a seaport or coast town.

Perhaps the strong resistance which the evangelical movement
was meeting there was the main reason why this great area was
left to so few workers.

The chronicle of the following years indicates that although
there were some encouragements, many of the same problems continued and the difficulties did not abate. Several new channels
of service were opened. A colporteur was employed. He sold
Christian literature in the market of Tampico in the mornings
and made visits during the afternoon hours. As he tried to
sell the Word of God he was persecuted, yet he persevered. A
girls' school was opened in Tampico with two resident lady
missionaries. A church was organized in Ciudad del Maiz after
several years of extreme opposition with fifteen members. An
orphanage was begun in Rioverde, San Luis Potosi with a new
missionary couple in charge and a medical mission work had
been established. However, there was trouble with the Roman
Catholics, the general economic state of Mexico caused an unrest and there was still much internal dissension.

By 1903 there were ten American missionaries on the field.
Work now covered three states - Tamaulipas, Vera Cruz and San
Luis Potosi. School and orphanage work was established and
preaching was being done in a number of different points. It
seemed that the time of reaping was near. The outlook for the
Church was bright and the Rev. S. W. Haddon speaking at the
centennial observance of the A. R. Presbyterian Church on
"Associate Reformed Presbyterians and Missions" was moved to
quote Bishop J. M. Thoburn:

> The signs of the times, the lessons of the past, the
> indications of the future, the call of providence, and
> the voices which come borne to us by every breeze, and
> from every nation under heaven, all alike bid us lay
> our plans upon a scale worthy of men who expect to
> conquer a world (Galloway 1905:691).

The next decade was a prosperous one for the missionary
endeavor in Mexico, but still there were difficulties. Evangelicals were despised and the fanaticism of the Roman Catholic Church was hard to overcome. Protestantism seemed to
spread chiefly among the poor. Those from the upper class
sneered at the "hallelujah's" as they called the Protestants,
ridiculing their faith and their works. The customs of the
country made the observance of the Lord's Day very difficult.
Work and trade ran counter to rest, worship and prayer. An
anti-American spirit prevalent in the country was on occasion
brought to bear against the missionaries. Many people had
lost confidence in any type of religion because of some of
the practices of the Roman Catholic Church. Against the

liberalism permitted there stood the high standards of the
Gospel of Jesus Christ. And one of the main difficulties was
that of superstition. It abounded everywhere and placed
barriers wherever the Christian faith was sown.

> Among the lower classes superstition is rife. To hang
> about the neck tiny images renders them immune to all
> evil spirits. A tiny Christ on the cross is placed in
> the mouth of the dying soul which helps it pass safely
> through the gates of glory ... And even after our mem-
> bers have been converted from these follies, the super-
> stitious ideas still cling to them and tend to choke
> the good seed of truth (Dale 1910:201,204).

A further discussion of the folk beliefs so prevalent among
the Mexican people can be found in Chapter III and by reading
the book by William Madsen listed in the bibliography.

On the other hand there were many encouragements. In 1912
the Board reported to the Synod: "No period in the history of
this (Mexican) work has been apparently so prosperous" (Kennedy 1951:605). There were churches, chapels and preaching
stations. We had primary and secondary schools, a boys
school with a theological department, an orphanage and a very
efficient hospital. A large number of national workers and
fifteen American missionaries were on the field. And the
chief encouragement came from the converts themselves. There
was an evidence of true spirituality among them as they exem-
plified the words of the Apostle Paul in II Corinthians 5:17
(R. S. V.):

> Therefore if any man be in Christ, he is a new crea-
> ture: old things are passed away; behold all things
> are become new.

Furthermore they evidenced the true spirit of evangelism as
the new converts sought out others to lead them to the Saviour.
They were loyal to their faith and above all to the Word of
God.

This situation is corroborated by quotes from the reports
of the missionaries on the field as they appeared in the
annual reports to the Synod and were printed in the minutes
of that body. Dr. Pressly had this to say:

> The gospel must be preached, duties are ours, results
> are God's ... Right here in Tampico, there is no
> Sabbath, no Sabbath School, no preaching of the Word;
> in the Romish church not five per centum of the people
> go to church, and not two per centum with any

regularity (Associate Reformed Presbyterian Church 1908: 64).

Mr. Hunter added:

> Rev. G. Cruz has been faithful in his ministerial appointments. He said, 'Tell the brethern that the people do not tear up the tracts and insult me as formerly, but often ask for something good to read, and make many inquiries about the religion (Associate Reformed Presbyterian Church 1908:65).

Mr. Dale mentioned the spiritual growth:

> As a result of these special services (held in Rioverde) fifteen persons were received into the Church on profession of their faith in Christ. The entire congregation was stirred to a deeper and better life for the Master (Associate Reformed Presbyterian Church 1909:53).

The period of prosperity was not to last however. In 1913 the Presbytery of Tampico "recorded with a heavy heart the saddest chapter in its history" (Kennedy 1951:605). Mexico was embroiled in the Revolution and the following year all of the missionaries were recalled to the United States. Some of them never returned. Dr. and Mrs. N. E. Pressly left in April, 1914 and returned in October of that same year. During this period of internal fighting, congregations were scattered, church property was destroyed and the native ministers became refugees. Many are the stories of the hardships they had to endure and of the things they were forced to do contrary to their beliefs.

Had it not been for the fact that the Church which had had such a promising beginning was not merely a human effort, our missionary endeavor in Mexico would surely have been ended by the Revolution. But the difficulties and hardships brought about by the Revolution fostered a spirit of self-support and self-government and spiritual values although sometimes kept under cover remained strong.

WORK AMONG THE INDIANS

Return of the Dales in 1919

After the unwanted furlough brought about as a result of the Revolution some of the missionaries returned to the field to see how the missionary effort could be resumed. The return

was gradual and they encountered many changes and many difficulties. Among the first to return were J. G. Dale and his
wife Dr. Katherine Neel Dale. They located in Tampico because
circumstances for their return to Rioverde, S. L. P. were not
favorable. In Tampico they discovered that the Revolution had
practically destroyed the mission on the coast and the two remaining churches had decided to separate from the A. R. P.
Mission. The Lord blessed their efforts there, however, and
at the end of an eleven year period the Dales had organized in
Tampico five churches with a membership of eight hundred fifty-
one. As Mr. Dale said: "Mightily grew the Word of the Lord
and prevailed" (1943:99).

God's Call Into Indianland

The Dales, however, felt that the Lord was calling them to
a new field of service and were led to leave the work on the
coast to minister to the Indians. According to the Mexican
government there were five million Indians in Mexico at that
time (1930). The Aztec tribe had a population of 517,000.
The missionary effort had reached many commercial centers and
smaller towns, but the Dales thought of the many Indians who
had never had the chance to hear the good news of salvation.

In April, 1934 the Pioneer Mission Agency of Philadelphia
contacted the Board of Foreign Missions of the A. R. P. Church
to ask for the services of the Dales. The Board was willing
for the Dales to undertake this task, but felt that they were
unable to underwrite the expense of opening a new field although they did continue to pay Dr. Katherine Dale's salary.
Therefore, trusting in the Lord, they organized the Mexican
Indian Mission and were sponsored by the Pioneer Mission
Agency of Philadelphia, an interdenominational mission agency.
Missionary operations were opened at Tamazunchale, S. L. P.
and from that center they sought to evangelize the Aztecs.

The mission endeavor in Indianland was later separated from
that of the A. R. P. Church and the Presbytery of Tampico as
support came from two different boards. The majority of the
Indians residing within the area compassed by our Church remained untouched until some years later when evangelistic
efforts were begun among the Aztec and Huastec tribes. A more
prolonged discussion of this ministry can be found in Chapter
VI.

2

Encouraging Aspects in the Development of the Church

STATISTICS OF NINETY YEARS

The A. R. P. Mission has completed ninety years of ministry in Mexico. Plate 3 presents a statistical picture of the growth of our Chruch during those years. The graph gives the appearance that the Church has been growing at an acceptable rate with the exception of two periods. Yet a closer analysis alters the initial impression. Read, Monterosso and Johnson in their monumental study on the growth of the Church in Latin America give the following figures for Mexico: the current annual population growth rate is 3.5 per cent and the annual growth rate for all evangelicals from 1960-1967 was 11 per cent (1969:49). The Associate Reformed Presbyterian Church shows only an average annual increase for 1960-1969 of 2.4 per cent. This is less than the average rate of biological growth which means growth taking place from those born into Christian families. Note that the average rate of growth for the entire ninety year period has been 5.5 per cent. It is common to scorn church statistics, but there is nothing particularly spiritual in ignoring them and certainly they are essential to understanding church growth.

What have other evangelical churches done in the area served by our denomination? As we have noted, our ministry covers a part of the three states of Tamaulipas, San Luis Potosi and Vera Cruz. The charts of the individual states (Plates 4, 6 and 8) indicate the location of organized A. R. P. Churches and with a different symbol where there are only preaching points. The bar graphs (Plates 5, 7 and 9) portray the work of other denominations and boards in the same area, with a comparison of the membership figures of each. Note the middle position occupied by our Church in all three states.

It is hoped that a review of these statistics will give us
a picture of how the national Church has developed during the
ninety years since our first missionary set foot on Mexican
soil. There have been many encouraging aspects in the development, yet admittedly the A. R. P. Church in Mexico would be
classified as a static Church. It is imperative then, being
confronted with this fact, that we analyze the factors that
have influenced the development and those that have deterred
the growth. Our emphasis in this chapter will be on the elements which have produced growth. Later information will deal
with the discouraging factors. We desire to discover those
ingredients which will lead to the numerical, spiritual and
organic growth of our Church. We invite you to share our
concern.

FACTORS INFLUENCING GROWTH

One cannot begin to discuss the factors which have influenced growth in any given Church without a recognition of the
power and work of the Holy Spirit in the spread of Christianity.
In writing of the difficulties encountered in the A. R. P.
mission endeavor in Mexico it was said:

> Were foreign missions a merely human work, the debacle
> in Mexico would have in all probability ended our mission
> work for a generation (Kennedy 1951:606).

But through faith in Christ and courage given by the Holy
Spirit the early missionaries persevered. In looking at the
entire spectrum of church history, Basil Matthews has written
of the same type of courageous perseverance:

> Paul and Peter, Martin of Tours and Patrick, Columba,
> Boniface, and Francis Xavier, with other dauntless
> pioneers, unknown as well as famous, sailed the upper
> reaches of that river whose waters still flow past our
> doors. That stream, which always 'keeps rolling along,'
> is the ongoing life of 'the holy church throughout all
> the world' (1960:247).

Our hearts resound with praise as we stand within our own
Church, having an awareness that in spite of the human fail-
ings and mistakes, the Body of Christ has expanded. We have
heard echoed over and over again that glorious proclamation
of the Apostle Paul in Galatians 2:20 (R. S. V.):

> I have been crucified with Christ; it is no longer I

PLATE 3

ASSOCIATE REFORMED PRESBYTERIAN COMMUNICANT MEMBERSHIP

IN MEXICO 1881-1970

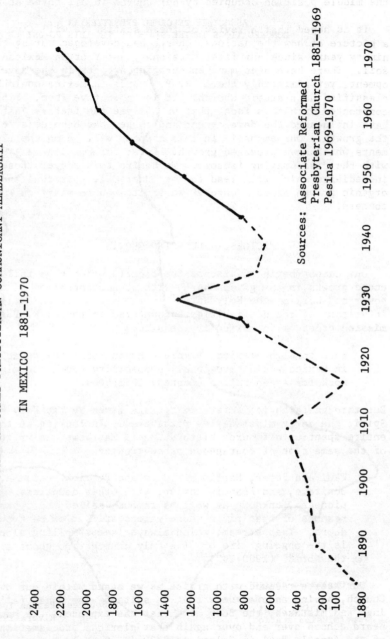

Sources: Associate Reformed
Presbyterian Church 1881-1969
Pesina 1969-1970

PLATE 4

ASSOCIATE REFORMED PRESBYTERIAN
CONGREGATIONS IN THE STATE OF SAN LUIS POTOSI
1970

Key:

° = Organized church

+ = Preaching point
    (mission station)

Sources: Pesina 1969-1970
         Rivera 1962

PLATE 5

COMMUNICANT MEMBERSHIP OF PROTESTANT CHURCHES
IN SAN LUIS POTOSI   1960

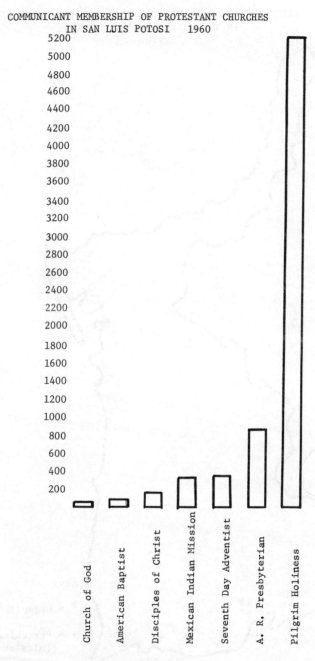

Sources: Taylor and Coggins 1961
        Associate Reformed Presbyterian Church 1961

PLATE 6

ASSOCIATE REFORMED PRESBYTERIAN CONGREGATIONS
IN THE STATE OF TAMAULIPAS
1970

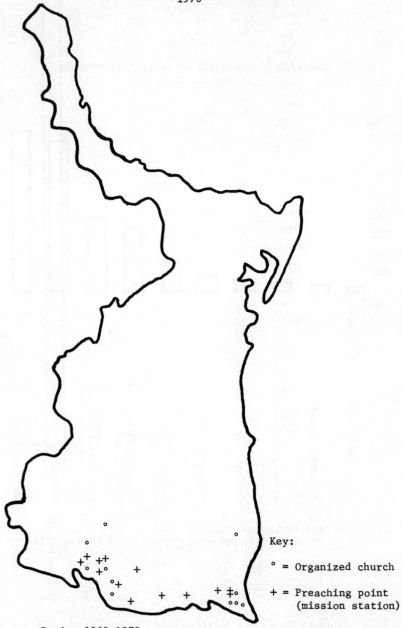

Key:

° = Organized church

+ = Preaching point
(mission station)

Sources: Pesina 1969-1970
Rivera 1962

PLATE 7

COMMUNICANT MEMBERSHIP OF PROTESTANT CHURCHES
IN TAMAULIPAS   1960

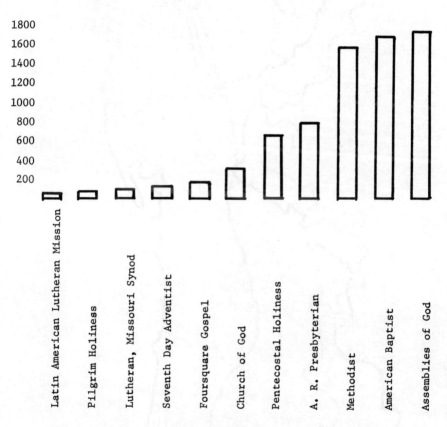

Sources: Taylor and Coggins 1961
         Associate Reformed Presbyterian Church 1961

PLATE 8

ASSOCIATE REFORMED PRESBYTERIAN CONGREGATIONS
IN THE STATE OF VERA CRUZ
1970

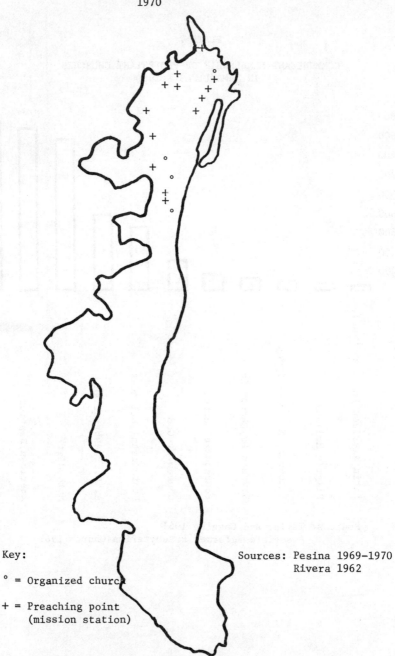

Key:

° = Organized church

+ = Preaching point
   (mission station)

Sources: Pesina 1969–1970
           Rivera 1962

PLATE 9

COMMUNICANT MEMBERSHIP OF PROTESTANT CHURCHES
IN VERA CRUZ   1960

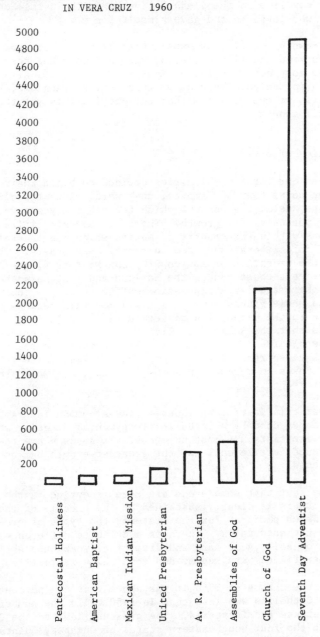

Sources: Taylor and Coggins 1961
         Associate Reformed Presbyterian Church 1961

who live, but Christ who lives in me; and the life I
now live in the flesh I live by faith in the Son of God,
who loved me and gave himself for me.

This newness of life as experienced by missionary and national,
by educated and illiterate, by rich and poor has been the
single most decisive factor in the growth of the A. R. P.
Church in Mexico. Even as we turn to more tangible, human
factors, we must realize that the spiritual is yet the basis
for all growth.

Location of Field

When our first missionaries decided to begin their ministry
in the coast town of Tampico, they were, without realizing it,
perhaps, selecting an area which through the years would have
great potential for growth. There are certain cities and
regions within the country of Mexico which are characteristi-
cally more liberal and open to change than others. These,
with the exception of Mexico City and Monterrey, are located
on the east coast and on the Mexican and Guatemalan borders.
Here there are large population shifts as people come and go
and as whole groups move from arrid mountain regions and re-
settle in the metropolis to seek a living. It is in such
places that the Roman Catholic Church has less influence and
the people feel less bound to follow a religion toward which
they have no real ties nor responsibilities. Life in these
areas takes on more of an anonymity and the atmosphere is
one of receptivity.

That this is true is shown in the accompanying map, results
of a study done by a Catholic clergyman, indicating where
the Protestants are most numerous. It shows where the Gospel
has found fertile soil and the greatest growth has been experienced.

The fact that some areas are more receptive to the Gospel
than others is clearly sustained in the parable of the sower.
Here Jesus pictures for the listener the types of ground into
which the seed falls. There is a definite difference in the
types of soil, some hard and dry, other rocky and shallow,
another filled with weeds, and some which is fertile.

In the census of 1960 it was shown that the percentage of
Roman Catholics was less than in 1950 while the number of
Protestants had increased. The greatest loss to the Catholics
was in the four southeastern states of Chiapas, Quintana Roo,
Campeche and Tabasco which border with Guatemala. Second to
these came the gulf states and those of the northern border.

PLATE 10

DENSIDAD DE POBLACION
PROTESTANTE

DENSITY OF PROTESTANT POPULATION
IN MEXICO   1960

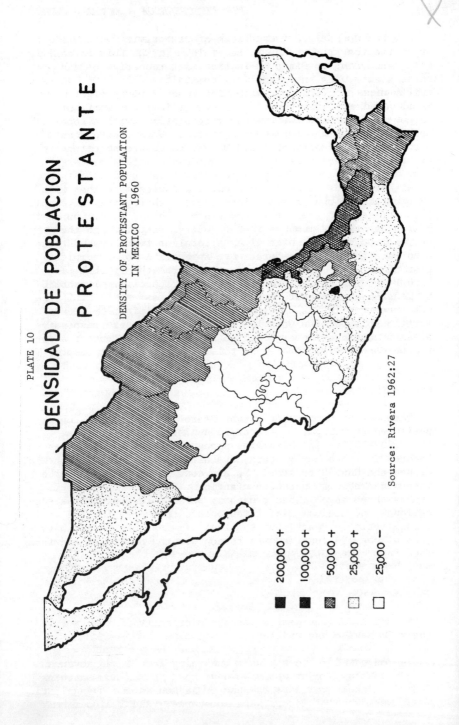

200,000 +

100,000 +

50,000 +

25,000 +

25,000 —

Source: Rivera 1962:27

Now let us analyze these facts of receptivity in the light
of statistics from the A. R. P. field. In San Luis Potosi,
which according to Plate 10 is the least receptive of the
three states with an evangelical community of 25,000+, we have
thirty-nine congregations with nine hundred forty-eight members. In Tamaulipas there is an evangelical community of
50,000+ and we have twenty-four congregations with a total
membership of eight hundred ninety-two. Vera Cruz has an
evangelical community of 100,000+ and there are seventeen
A. R. P. congregations with five hundred nineteen members.
Although there are a few more members in San Luis Potosi than
in either of the other two states, statistics show that with
49 per cent of the congregations located there, they have only
33.5 per cent of the total membership. The A. R. P. Church in
Mexico has thirty members in the Federal District and the
state of Guanajuato which gives a total of two thousand three
hundred eighty-nine members. See Appendix A for a complete
list of churches. These facts sustain the theory that the
border and coastal states are the most receptive. It should
be mentioned also that in February, 1970, an A. R. P. Church
was organized in Mexico City which had traditionally been
fertile soil for the Gospel. A knowledge of these responsive
areas should provide a guideline for our future concentration.
A more complete discussion on this will be found in Chapter VI.

Church Planting Missionaries

Note on the membership graph (Plate 3) that the Church experienced an 8.2 per cent average annual rate of increase
from 1902-1910. The hardships among which the missionaries
labored in those early years have already been discussed. What
caused the Church to grow? We are convinced that it was the
vigorous emphasis on church planting. By 1910 there were
twenty-three established preaching points. Certainly the educational and medical ministries opened the doors for the
evangelistic outreach, but the fact remains that the primary
goal of the missionaries was to convert the nationals and form
them into churches.

Use of Laymen

Robert A. Whitesides, a veteran missionary of twenty-five
years in Mexico has written:

> You asked me to say what one thing I felt had advanced
> our church most while we have been in Mexico. I think
> my answer would be the use of laymen in the evangelistic
> work when ministers were so scarce. And I also firmly

believe that further growth is going to depend more and
more on the participation of more and more Mexican laymen in the work of the church (1969: Letter to author).

The preaching force of our Church in Mexico is largely made
up of laymen. They have gone forth with their faith and the
Bible and have been the backbone of leadership in our denomination. Without these men and women the extension of our
Church would be seriously hindered.

In addition to the laymen who serve in a preaching capacity
there are those within the membership of the Church who have
contributed significantly in the development. One of these is
the *Sociedad Femenil*. There are more than twenty societies of
women in the A. R. P. field and each group has a positive program of outreach. It is expressed in actively providing leadership for another preaching point in some suburb of the city,
in holding weekly evangelistic services and Bible study groups
in the jail, in a program of visitation and in a ministry of
prayer.

Another very active group is that of the young people, the
Esfuerzo Cristiano. The name itself, "the Christian Force,"
signifies what the young people are to the church and the
community in which they live. Their enthusiasm for the
Christian faith has time and time again helped bring others
into the fellowship of the Church. They make up much of the
actual leadership. This was evidenced recently when a group
of young leaders met to discuss what could be done to win and
strengthen those in the intermediate group, ages 12 to 14.
After a planning session they formulated a workable plan and
are in 1970 putting it into practice.

These, as well as Spirit filled individuals within the
Church, have been and will continue to be a positive element
in the ongoing of the Kingdom of God in Mexico.

Program of Christian Education

In the reports coming in over the years from missionaries
in the Mexican field, one fact has stood out in relation to
church growth. In the sections where there has been an active
and well formulated program of Christian education the Church
has experienced growth. The Sunday School work was the main
emphasis of the single ladies in the early years. This with
a corresponding plan of home visitation was credited with
bringing many into the Church. This is true today.

Christian education in the area of Vacation Bible Schools

has also been a factor in the growth of the Church. Parents
are more willing to allow their children to attend programs
such as these. There are numerous examples of entire families
coming into the membership of the Church due to this reason.
In one urban congregation at least three of the families were
won through the Vacation Bible School.

The only danger involved and the breakdown to be avoided is
winning the children without the parents. It is in this realm
that the follow-up is of utmost importance. With a child or
children already actively involved in the church, the door of
the home is open and the climate is one of receptivity. That
this can be used to advantage has been proved in a number of
our city churches. That it has been neglected can also be
seen, particularly in the rural areas where often almost the
entire congregation is made up of children.

Institutes and Evangelistic Campaigns

The A. R. P. Mission conducts on an annual basis institutes
for the paid lay workers. The site varies as the needs of the
congregations are considered. A place is selected where the
church seems to have difficulty growing and where a potential
response is believed to be present. The objective, of course,
is to provide the lay worker with training in principles and
methods to aid him in his work. An underlying goal, however,
is an evangelistic lift to the host church. The entire group
is involved in this latter goal as they use the method of personal witness throughout the period. The enthusiasm generated
in such institutes has been a factor in church growth.

Another positive effort has been the evangelistic campaigns
led by a team of nationals with one missionary which goes by
invitation to any area on the field. The campaigns are set up
for three days. The daylight hours are occupied with a program of house-to-house visitation for the purpose of making
the acquaintance of every family in the village and of per-
sonally inviting them to the nightly services. All types of
Christian literature are offered for sale. It has been observed that free literature is regarded of little worth, while
on the other hand something that costs must be of value. The
time following the first service is used in a follow-up program
of visitation making use of the local baptized believers as
well as the team members. Many decisions for Christ have come
out of such campaigns, but here again the problem of post-
baptismal instruction is evident if the full potential for
growth is to be realized. Several factors would be included
in this instruction: a study of the Bible by the literate
members, memorization of portions of Scripture by the illiterate,

training for the laymen, teaching the illiterate to read the
Bible and involving all in a program of witness to their
friends and neighbors.

National Leadership

The membership graph (Plate 3) shows that the most con-
sistent and steady increase has been from 1945 until the
present time. The emerging national leadership has contributed to this trend. Mrs. R. A. Whitesides has said:

> Our Bible School for the first time in years produced a
> goodly number of ministers -- Amador Pesina, Don Chon
> Juarez, Ruben Castaneda, Ezequiel Gallegos, and
> Guillermo Peruyero -- to take their places of leader-
> ship. These were another generation, a generation of
> ideas and willing to fight for a Mexican church (1969:
> Letter to author).

The Presbytery of Tampico which had been organized in the
first decade of our missionary endeavor in Mexico making the
Mexican denomination only a branch of the mother Church was
in 1964 dramatically changed. The one Presbytery became
three, one for each of the states where there are churches,
and a separate and independent *Sinodo Presbiteriano Asociado
Reformado de Mexico* was organized. It was a highlight in the
life of the Church as it spotlighted the national Church and
recognized the efforts and leadership of the Mexican ministers.

Heightened Expectations

Dr. Donald McGavran in writing of the elements which make
for growing churches has said:

> The missions in Mexico, which between 1880 and 1940 met
> with scant response, great persecution, and terrible
> prejudice, learned by bitter experience to cultivate
> low expectations ... But the curve of Evangelical church
> growth in Mexico shows a rocket-like upsurge in the last
> 20 years (1963:64).

Our own denomination has grown from 922 in 1945 to 2,389 in
1969. This is evidence that the responsiveness of Mexico has
been altered. There is an air of expectance of growth where
before there had been contentment with the status quo. The
personality of the Protestant community is showing a new side
without the apologies and shame which formerly marked many of
the evangelicals.

True there is still persecution and ridicule in some sections. As late as 1968 when the author was in the state of
San Luis Potosi with an evangelistic team to hold a three day
series of special services in a small village, a group of
reactionaries came to run us out of town. There were some
twenty men from the Roman Catholic Church who contended that
the Protestants had no right to be proclaiming the Gospel in
that town and in fact were not needed nor wanted there. After
a lengthy discussion we did continue with the services. Yet
such occurances as these are on the decrease, occuring only
in such areas where the sentiment and loyalty are still
strongly Roman Catholic.

In other parts of Mexico, the climate is changing to one
of responsiveness. Several examples quite vividly point out
this trend. The A. R. P. Church in Mante has expressed an
interest in church music under the leadership of the author.
In recent years the church choir has been invited to present
a program of sacred music on the radio station in Ciudad
Valles, S. L. P. and to play on the station in Mante a tape
of a concert presented in many of our churches. Such "adver-
tisement" for the Church would not have been possible twenty
years ago. Although regrettably never carried out, plans for
a public Christmas concert in the main plaza of Mante were
approved by the town council. This new willingness to accept
the Protestants and indeed to listen to them must certainly
be given credit for much of the growth in the immediate past.

All of this is a strong indication that the gradualism
which marked much of the mission approach in past decades
must be abandoned in order to take advantage of the new climate which expects growth. It no longer is feasible nor wise
simply to carry on that which we have, but rather an expec-
tant, vigorous effort must be made to reach the unchurched
with the message of redemption, to reach them in great numbers
as rapidly as possible and to place them in churches.

> Whole countries in various parts of the world, from
> time to time, become so responsive, in comparison with
> their former indifference, that a new dimension of
> church growth and a new kind of church planting become
> possible. When this occurs, under the mighty hand of
> God, Christian mission should turn from the expecta-
> tions, methods, and proportions which suited the former
> days of indifference and embrace the expectations,
> images, and emphasis suited to planting churches in the
> fruitful contemporary scene (McGavran 1965a:14).

GROWTH OF A TYPICAL URBAN CHURCH

In our denomination, the churches which have shown the
most potential for growth, particularly in recent years, have
been those in the cities. An example of one such urban congregation is that of the *Iglesia P. A. R. Príncipe de Paz*
located in Ciudad Mante, Tamaulipas. Mante has a population
of approximately 50,000 and there are several other Protestant denominations with churches there. The A. R. P. Church
is, however, the largest of these in membership. The following graph pictures the growth of this church.

The A. R. P. ministry in the Mante area was begun around
1934 when Miss Janie Love organized the

> Mision Huasteca and visited such places as Nuevo More-
> los, El Pachon, El Abra, Quintero, *Ciudad Mante,* San
> Rafael de los Castro, El Meco, El Pensil, Chamal City,
> Rancho Nuevo, El Sinai, etc. (Gallegos n.d.:4).

From 1934-1942 occasional visits were made to Mante by Miss
Love along with several national workers whom she had trained.
The majority of these received no salary. The first services
were held in private homes, one of these being that of the
Sra. Julia Ch. de Garcia. Sra. Garcia was a member of the
A. R. P. Church in Tamanzunchale, S. L. P. and had moved to
Mante. In writing of her contribution to the development of
the church it was said:

> You could hardly find a better example of love and of
> dedication to the Lord's work. She helped Miss Love in
> the work at Quintero and especially the work here (Cd.
> Mante) (Gallegos n.d.:5).

Mrs. Garcia could not read, but her zeal for Christian
testimony was unparalleled. She was always ready to speak to
any group about the Gospel. She would simply ask someone in
the congregation to read a passage of Scripture and then she
would explain it. Her gift of wisdom imparted by the Holy
Spirit more than made up for her lack of literary accomplishments. Along with Senorita Daria Ponce, Sra. Garcia rented
a house and the two women were in charge of the Mante mission.

The next step in the growth of the tiny congregation from
1942 to 1947, was a period during which resident paid lay
workers attended the mission. One of these was the husband
of Srita. Ponce. His enthusiasm and interest in the spread
of the Gospel are noted by one outstanding phase of his
ministry. He held a special service each Sunday at 4:00 a.m.
for the merchants who had to go to work at 6:00 or 7:00 a.m.

PLATE 11

COMMUNICANT MEMBERSHIP OF THE *PRINCIPE DE PAZ* ASSOCIATE
REFORMED PRESBYTERIAN CHURCH, CIUDAD MANTE, TAMAULIPAS, MEXICO
1950–1970

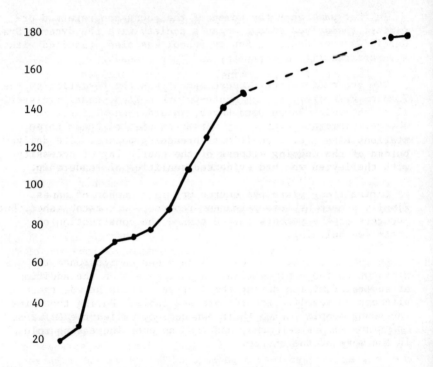

Source: Gallegos n.d.

In spite of the inconvenient hour, many attended the services.
The problem of the celebration of the Lord's Day is still present today. Sunday is perhaps the biggest commercial day of
the week. It is the time when the ranch people all go to town
to purchase their weekly supplies and the stores do their
biggest business.

In 1947 with the death of Miss Love who had been supervising
the Mante mission, the congregation passed under the care of
the Presbytery of Tampico. That body continued to supply the
preaching point with paid lay workers.

In that same year the women of the young congregation organized themselves into a woman's society with the dynamic Sra.
Garcia as president. A Sunday School was also organized with
a superintendent, a secretary and four classes.

The succeeding step of development was the formation by the
Tampico Presbytery of the Mante-Quintero-Xicotencatl ministerial circuit with Ramon Orta Reyes, an ordained minister in
charge. Together with a lay worker he visited these three
stations plus twelve additional preaching points. The daily
burden of the ongoing witness of the church lay of necessity
with the laymen who had evidenced qualities of leadership.

During these years the church met in a number of homes.
Finally a more or less permanent residence was established, but
thoughts of the members turned toward the construction of
their own building.

In 1949 Sr. Ascension de la Tejera was commissioned to
minister to the congregation. Accounts mention the addition
of several families during the fourteen months he was there
although no specific records are available. During that time
the young people formed their own society called the *Esfuerzo
Cristiano Amigos de Jesus,* and took an ever increasing role
in the work of the church.

The church had its first resident ordained minister in 1950
when Rev. Ramon O. Reyes took up the pastorate. During his
ministry a lot on Zaragoza Street was purchased for the amount
of $5,000m.n. and a building costing $30,000m.n. was constructed
in three months. This is the present locale of the church.
Note on Plate 11 that the church had twenty members at that
time.

At the close of that memorable year the Home Mission Board
of Tampico Presbytery sent a young man named Amador Pesina
Gonzalez to take charge of the work.

It was then that was begun what has been until the present
time and will surely continue to be a brillant ministry
(Gallegos n.d.: 10).

By special petition, Pesina, a graduate of the Bible School in
Rioverde, was ordained on March 22, 1952, thus becoming the
official minister with all the rights, privileges and responsibilities thereof. He continues at present as minister of the
congregation. An outstanding Christian leader, he has with great
insight and much spiritual wisdom guided this young church.

On October 26, 1952, the Mante Church was officially organized in a moving service. Rev. Guillermo Peruyero and Elder
Ascension de la Tejera were the official representatives of
the Presbytery of Tampico which in turn was under the auspicies
of the General Synod of the A. R. P. Church in the United
States. Forty persons signed the *Acta Constitutiva*. A large
number were attending church at that time, but only twenty-
eight were communicant members. Note on Plate 11 how the membership began to climb following the formal organization of
the church.

An outstanding factor in the growth of the church has been
the initiative taken by the members in self-government. The
first session was formed in 1952 with two ordained elders.
When one of these moved away from town only a few months later,
the congregation found it necessary to form a **governing** board
which consisted of two men and three women. In the absence of
qualified men to serve as ruling elders, many of our churches
have had to resort to the use of a governing board on which
the women play an important part.

This board functioned until 1957. At that time the Suarez
children attended the Vacation Bible School and later other
activities of the church. Mr. Pesina visited with the parents
and as a result Sr. Moises Suarez, his wife, and entire family
of eleven children came into the church. Sr. Suarez brought
with him, in addition to his family, a tremendous amount of
enthusiasm and dedication. Within a year he was elected as
ruling elder and from that date until the present, the session
has continued to function.

Another man came into the church by marrying a Christian
girl. Sr. Jaime Torres Garcia was a man of liberal ideas, but
was not a converted believer. His wife-to-be finally persuaded him to agree to be married in the A. R. P. Church following the civil ceremony which is required by law in Mexico.
The church wedding has religious significance only. The young
liberal consented on one condition - that he would not have to
kneel at any time during the ceremony. The session agreed and
the two ceremonies were completed without further ado. Jaime

Torres began to frequent the church and little by little his attitude changed. He soon accepted Christ as Lord and Saviour, becoming a member of the church. Thus about a year after his marriage the new believer was ordained as an elder and the session had three members.

At the same time Sr. Juan C. Saavedra also was ordained as elder. He had moved to Mante from Tampico where he was a member of the Vergel A. R. P. Church. Not finding his denominational group he had first gone to a Baptist Church in Mante, but under the witness and ministry of Mr. Pesina he soon joined the A. R. P. congregation where he has contributed much as a leader and in the field of music.

The enthusiasm radiated by the various groups and organizations of the church has been important. A large number of the members have been involved in the carrying out of these tasks through such agencies as the Sunday School, the woman's society, the youth, intermediate and children's groups, the choir and the different commissions elected by the church to serve for a year's time.

A large part of the membership could be classified as middle class with the remainder coming from the lower class. Remarkably they found a common ground on which to meet and to serve through their kinship in the Lord Jesus Christ. Leaders are found in both classes and it is these Spirit-filled individuals who provide the spark of outreach which is necessary for the extension of the Church, the Body of Christ. Such a person is Sra. Abundia C. Vda. de Korrodi. She has very little schooling and is economically quite poor, yet she is rich spiritually. Her faith is expressed in a jail ministry and in a personal witness throughout the city. The examples of others who have in the past and who still today express a similar faith are numerous.

The church, seeing a need for the Gospel in nearby areas, had had a part in four preaching stations, supplying the money and the personnel. One of these has been organized into a church. Three are still under the supervision of the mother congregation.

In synthesis, several factors are discernible in the growth of this urban congregation after 1951. It was in a growing town. From a small ranch Mante has in fifty years become a thriving city with a population of 50,000. It is a liberal city. Located in the state of Tamaulipas and only one hundred miles inland from the Gulf of Mexico, the Roman Catholic Church has accepted the Protestant movement, giving no persecution. Ten other denominations are in the city and the

percentage of Christians in the state is one in thirty, a fact
which increases responsiveness. The missionary who began the
work did not invest a great deal of foreign funds. We note
that paid lay workers were not used in the very beginning. The
nationals did most of the work. The church soon became self-
supporting and began contributing to Synod. A program of outreach was a part of the ministry.

Needless to say, the road has not always been easy and the
church has not always evidenced the success one might gather
from this story. Note on the graph (Plate 11) that there has
been a plateau since 1961. Young people have married non-
Christians and drifted away from the church. Others have moved
to different places. Yet the church has grown and still stands
firm as witness to her Lord in 1970. The grain field is white
unto the harvest even today and the prospects for the future
are bright if the church can begin to move again. The danger
always is that once the church is no longer accustomed to new
people coming in they may become sealed off and grow only at a
biological rate which is essentially what has taken place since
1961.

   Unless a congregation makes conscious effort at moving
   its members towards the nuclear pole, they will slowly
   drift in the opposite direction to nominality. This is
   a common problem with second-generation congregations on
   the mission field. We must continually keep in mind that
   each new generation must be won for Christ (Tippett 1966:
   13).

3

Discouraging Aspects in the Development of the Church

A look at the development of the A. R. Presbyterian Church in Mexico must of necessity include a study of those years and areas where there has been little or no growth. Dr. Donald McGavran in speaking of this has written:

> Numerical increase is not the only criterion of success. Other matters must be taken into account. Church development is like that of a child. Adequate nutrition, a maturing social awareness, and intelligence are desirable elements in development; but ... to disregard weight as a chief criterion is fatal (1966:16).

Even so, the growth of a Church is a healthy indication as to whether it is developing in other ways as well. We cannot ignore the need for growth nor must we fail to realize and evaluate those things which are hindering the expansion of the Body of Christ.

We do this with the understanding that growth in quality and quantity normally go together.

> Church growth includes both horizontal growth in numbers won to Christ, and verticle growth in depth of commitment of these people to God and to the way of Christ. Ideally, these two operate conjunctively, because growth only in numbers produces baptized pagans; growth only in "quality" leads to sterility and dead churches--keeping the form of Christianity but lacking the power of Christ (Olson 1969: 19).

It is a desire for this dual expansion and deepening in the

faith which forces us to probe into our own mission history
and search out those elements which have slowed and even on
occasion stopped our growth.

THE REVOLUTION AND THE FIRST DECLINE

Our Church has had two periods of decline in membership.
The first one was during the Revolution from 1910 - 1921. As
seen by the accompanying graph, the membership decreased to
almost nothing. No concrete statistics are available for that
period due to the turbulent conditions within the country and
the lack of communication, however, an estimate of the number
of communicants was made. Described by missionary and national
alike as one of the most dismal chapters in the history of the
Church, that decade was a time of confusion and death for
Mexico.

During the Díaz era (1876 - 1910) the poor were greatly
oppressed. The illiteracy rate was high, over 90 per cent of
the people owned no property and unjust procedures flourished
on all sides. The government favored foreign interests and
many immigrants were encouraged to enter Mexico, bringing with
them foreign capital. Although there was relative peace, the
masses were discontented as the gap between the rich and the
poor continued to widen and the situation worsened.

The spark of discontentment flamed into revolution when
Francisco I. Madero, favoring political and agrarian reforms,
announced his decision for candidacy to replace Díaz as
president of Mexico. Díaz decided not to hold the elections
and as a result violence erupted with Madero forming an army
to overthrow the Díaz regime. His philosophy was: "The
Mexican does not want bread; he wants liberty to earn bread"
(Cumberland 1968:243).

Just as a train on a downgrade gains momentum and the cars
break up in every direction, so the revolution rushed forward.
The momentum and the ideals which Madero advanced caused the
common people quickly to join him and the fight was on.

The fighting of the Madero forces against Díaz was not the
entire picture, however. The people began to wonder which
side would win and to ask the question what was in all this
for them. Many smaller groups began fighting each other as
well as against the Díaz and Madero armies. The names of
Pancho Villa, Carranza, Obregon and others were heard on the
lips of the people as the confusion spread. Bandits raided
towns and villages with no purpose other than picking up food
and money. Blood ran freely as some men killed because of

PLATE 12

DECLINE IN COMMUNICANT MEMBERSHIP OF THE
ASSOCIATE REFORMED PRESBYTERIAN CHURCH OF MEXICO
DURING THE REVOLUTION   1910-1920

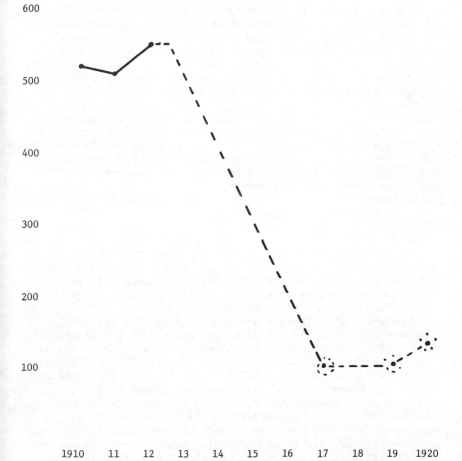

Source: Associate Reformed Presbyterian Church 1910-1921

their convictions and others for sheer pleasure. The government changed hands frequently.

This complicated period of the Revolution came to an end on
February 5, 1917 when the constitution of 1917 was proclaimed.
This great revolutionary document embodied the goals and purposes for which internal fighting had been constantly waging
since 1910.

During this chaotic period many of our churches were burned
or badly abused. Some of the members were killed and others
were scattered all over Mexico. Many were never to reunite
with the A. R. P. Church again. Tampico, the center of our
mission activity, was considered one of the safest places during
the Revolution. Yet even there we had nothing left in 1919
when the fires of fighting began to abate.

> When the Dales reached Tampico in 1919 they found that the
> revolution had destroyed all the churches of that field
> on the coast. Only the two congregations in the city
> (Tampico) remained and these had caught the nationalistic
> spirit so contagious at that time and had separated from
> their mother church and had declared themselves inde-
> pendent of all ecclesiastical affiliations (Dale 1943:
> 98-99).

With nothing left in the Tampico area and with conditions in
the interior of the country still unsettled, a new beginning
was the order of the day. No records of membership are available for the other churches, but the total number of communicants has been estimated at one hundred.

Related to the fighting and chaos was another factor that
was significant to the decrease: the absence of the missionary
force. Dr. and Mrs. Neill E. Pressly were only out of Mexico
for six months in 1914, but they were the only two until Miss
Macie Stevenson and Miss Lavinia Neel arrived on the field in
1917. Dr. Pressly was at that time vice-consul of Tampico, a
position which enabled him to stay on the field during most of
the Revolution although in rather a dangerous situation. He
was unable to leave the city to see what was happening in the
churches he had planted in the surrounding countryside and no
communication lines were open. Services were held with regularity in the city of Tampico and many attended, but with total
unrest it was difficult to plant a normal Church.

Dr. W. W. Boyce who served on our mission field for two
short periods, one before and one after the Revolution, feels
that several things hindered church growth during that era.

"The Board didn't have authority, vision or money" (Boyce 1969: Interview). He also believes that the missionaries were sent ill-prepared. In his own case his ministry was hindered by his lack of proficiency in the language. Mexico today has several schools and institutes for the purpose of teaching Spanish to foreigners, but in the first quarter of the century these were not in existence.

As the missionary enters another culture with the ultimate aim of presenting the Gospel in such a way that many will be saved, he must be culturally sensitive, having an awareness of the factors of his location. He must know the language which in a real sense is the door to the thoughts and customs of a people. He must make use of all the modern means at his disposal to communicate the Gospel. He must be aware that within the culture of the country as a whole there are various shadings which make it necessary to use one method in one area with one segment of the population and another method in another area with a different type of people. Thus a good knowledge of the language becomes the gateway to a true understanding of the cultural environment and the way to work in it with the most effectiveness.

Dr. Boyce agreed that the growth of the Church was stunted because of the absence of the missionary personnel. The accompanying graph (Plate 13) sustains that theory: decrease in personnel is correlated to a fall in membership.

THE DEPRESSION AND A SECOND DECLINE

The second period of decrease in the membership of the Church was from 1930-1941. See graph (Plate 14) depicting this. The overwhelming external factor which played a part in this regression was the depression in the United States. In 1930 with the strained financial conditions on the home front, money was hard to raise. As a direct result the mission cause suffered.

Funds to the foreign field were reduced thus limiting the work of the missionaries. Salaries for the native workers which were being sent from the home board were slow in reaching Mexico as well as those for the missionaries themselves. No new missionaries were sent out at this time at all and death further reduced the number so that by 1946 only four were on the field.

The close correlation between the number of missionary personnel and the growth of the Church can be noted in Plate 13.

PLATE 13

CORRELATION OF COMMUNICANT MEMBERSHIP AND
MISSIONARY PERSONNEL OF THE ASSOCIATE REFORMED PRESBYTERIAN
CHURCH OF MEXICO   1881-1970

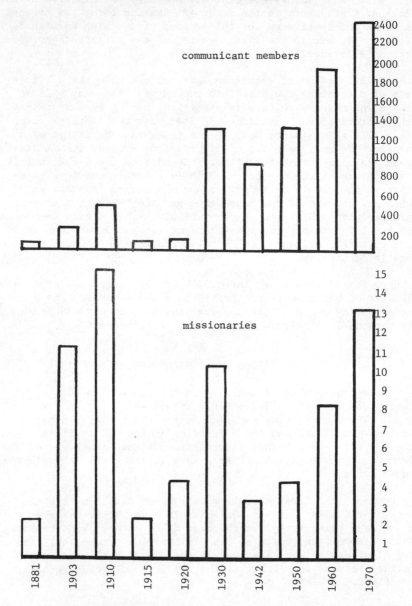

Sources: Kennedy 1951
         Associate Reformed Presbyterian Church 1881-1969
         Pesina 1969-1970

PLATE 14

DECLINE IN COMMUNICANT MEMBERSHIP OF
THE ASSOCIATE REFORMED PRESBYTERIAN CHURCH OF MEXICO
DURING THE DEPRESSION   1930-1941

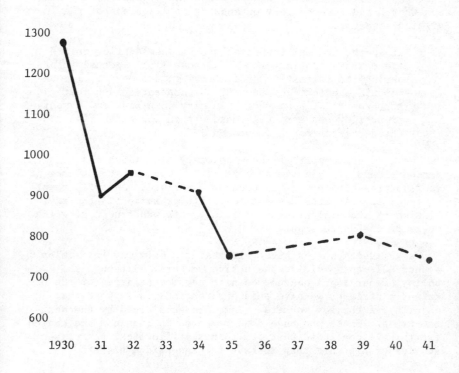

Source: Associate Reformed Presbyterian Church 1930-1941

As before the one is directly related to the other. Therefore,
just as the mission endeavor suffered during the Revolution
when the foreign workers were reduced, so a repetition of the
same thing occurred during the depression. Such a fact is
alarming. It has been noted that a prolonged control by missionaries has delayed church growth as the nationals have learned
to depend on them and the funds they bring with them rather
than on God. That such was the situation in our Church in the
1930's is vividly portrayed by what happened.

As funds were reduced from the home board, so the growth of
the Church became a mirror of the reduction, emphasizing the
fact that for many years, indeed since the beginning, the Mexican Church had come to rely on subsidy in all areas of the
mission endeavor.

> It is the unusual churchman who can use subsidy to aid
> the church-planting process without simultaneously hin-
> dering the initiative or destroying autonomy ... The un-
> fortunate effects of subsidy administration are felt
> throughout Latin America. In many countries employment
> of subsidy has seriously handicapped whole denominations
> (Read, Monterroso and Johnson 1969:363).

The hand of support of the missionary has always been extended financially in the support of lay workers who man the
various preaching points throughout our field. Any withdrawal
of funds in this area has seemed to hinder seriously the extension of the ministry and certainly this was true during the
years of the depression.

Many mission boards have felt that the only way to develop
a Church is to subsidize the native workers. Although the
policy of our Board has not been to pay the salaries of the ordained ministers, we have paid and continue to support the
majority of the lay workers. Some are subsidized by the Mexican Synod. Those who have done research in missions and church
growth have concluded that few things stifle local enthusiasm
and leadership more than to have foreign-paid ministers.

> Obviously no local church wishes to take on responsibility
> for a pastor's salary as long as the mission will provide
> it ... At the same time, the laity within a church may
> insist that, since the pastor is paid to do church work
> and they are not, all the work of the church is his re-
> sponsibility, and they are accordingly relieved of any
> necessity to witness or promote the cause (McGavran 1965b
> 184-185).

If it is felt that the Church cannot assume the full financial responsibility of the ministers and lay workers, it is best to help with indirect support, letting the local congregation handle the funds which are paid to the minister. Though not ideal, this type of support does not damage the local sense of responsibility and at the same time encourages the congregation to assume more and more of the support.

The missionaries on our field who have been responsible for the evangelistic effort over much of the Synod have felt that a program which is led and supported by the nationals is necessary and have formulated a proposal to put such into effect. This will be discussed at greater length in Chapter VI.

Although no statistics are available to verify how much the withdrawal of medical work could have affected the growth of the Church from 1930-1941, it should be noted that at that time Dr. Katherine Neel Dale went with her husband to work among the Indians. This left the A. R. P. mission field without a medical ministry. Doors had been closed by the authorities in Tampico and it seemed inadvisable to continue there. However, the medical effort had been a powerful force in reaching people for Christ and it must be assumed that its cessation would affect the growth of the Church to some extent.

> It was the clinic of Dr. Dale that had so much to do with this remarkable ingathering of souls (800 members in eight years). From 1919 and on through the years, crowds passed through her clinic. And those patients, numbering seventy and eighty each day, running into the thousands during the year, had heard the Bible read and its gospel explained ... Undoubtedly in Dr. Dale's clinic were generated influences that had much to do with the revival that stirred Tampico (Dale 1943:100-101).

OTHER OBSTACLES TO CHURCH GROWTH

In the overall statistical picture of the growth of the A. R. P. Church in Mexico it can be seen that there has been no one single period when the Church has extended rapidly. The two periods already mentioned were times of recession, but throughout the years the growth has been slow. Dr. McGavran has the following to say about plateaux in church growth:

> Arrested growth is seldom good mission policy. It comes about through lack of skill, or lack of resources or both. Plateaux in growth are usually made by man not ordained by God (1966:35).

What have been some of the elements within our Church and
Mission which have been responsible for the slow development
which has been experienced?

An American Church

One obstacle was the fact that the Church planted in Mexico
was essentially an American Church. Mrs. R. A. Whitesides
writing about this has said:

> When we came to Mexico 25 years ago, we saw organized
> churches that were just exactly alike whether in Rio
> Verde or Tampico. Their form of worship and the regular
> service were as much mission as if the missionary had
> been there to direct ... When a missionary goes out he
> has no other church but the home church to copy. This is
> natural. But it mustn't remain so if you are to have a
> growing church to meet the needs of the people in a
> different culture (1969: Letter to author).

Robert L. Brawley who has recently returned from a short
term of service in Mexico observed the same tendency. He noted:

> The early mission work, and practically all of it before
> the 1950's was to make the Mexicans like Southern ARP
> Americans. Some of this is still seen (Brawley 1970:
> Letter to author).

Dr. W. W. Boyce in speaking about the Church in the first
quarter of the twentieth century asserted that he felt the
Mission at that time was placing an unnecessary burden on the
national Church in seeking to make it like the home Church.
He mentioned to the Board that we should establish an autonomous Church, one that was more a part of the people and not so
dependent on the missionaries (Boyce 1969: Interview).

One type of cultural overhang that was particularly noticeable in the establishment of the Church was the fact that Psalm
singing was introduced. The singing of the Psalms has been a
part of the A. R. P. Church in the United States throughout
its history, and in the early years of mission work a portion
of the Psalter was translated into Spanish. In the ensuing
years various books were used until 1965 when Dr. W. C. Halliday published *Cantos Biblicos* which contains both psalms and
hymns. He was assisted in this labor by several of the national
Christians and the end result is a book which has added much to
the worship service.

Others have noted about the Protestant movement in general

that one of the obstacles to its growth was the extension of
the Church in the United States, forming Mexican Churches which
were almost literal reproductions.

> They sought to extend their own Church rather than to
> encourage a religious reform of a kind to be determined
> largely by local environment and needs (Baez Camargo and
> Grubb 1935:109).

It was this lack of awareness of the importance of the foreign
culture and the necessity of communicating the Gospel within the
culture that seriously hindered the growth of the A. R. P.
Church. The anthropologist H. G. Barnett has written that
missionaries often are conservers of the traditions of their
homeland. He goes further to state that it does not end there,
but they become advocates of its extension among the believers.

Particularly in the first half of the twentieth century was
this a serious obstacle in the A. R. P. Church. The nationals
spoke of their churches as being the congregations of a certain
beloved missionary who pioneered in the work in that section.
An Americanized Church had been transplanted into a Mexican
culture and the end result was slow growth.

A sharp reminder that perhaps this truth had been realized
by the nationals was voiced by Robert Brawley:

> Even after the establishment of an independent Synod, we
> managed to continue to rule the church from the mission-
> ary standpoint. It really hit me when Ruben Castaneda
> said in Synod of 1968: "You missionaries have been won-
> derful for us, you have truly been concerned for us. But
> why don't you ask us what we think is best for us' (1970:
> Letter to author).

Failure to Utilize People Movements

Some areas within our denomination show quite clearly the
picture of slow growth. Twenty-five preaching points each have
baptized communities of twelve or under. Some have been
opened recently, but in others the Gospel has been proclaimed
for at least ten years. Most are rural communities. One of
the main causes for this slow growth has been our failure to
use the communication lines which are open between family members. Ours has been a witness to individuals rather than a
witness to a people. We have failed to realize the cultural
significance of a group response. In "A Christian Movement
in Mexico" (Cowan 1962) the writer gives a graphic look at how
the Gospel was planted in one Indian village. A man from a

neighboring region had the opportunity to witness to a man and his son-in-law. Interest was generated and in further discussion including the entire family, a decision came. Sixteen asked for baptism and seven refused to accept. From this family the church spread through kinship channels and then through social channels. It is significant that all those who responded were within the same economic and ethnic group.

Although this example was of an Indian community, the situation in regard to family ties is similar in most rural villages in Mexico. Charles Bennett in analyzing the kinship structure in rural areas and its relation to conversion has written:

1. If the husband accepts first, the wife will follow ... *Se gana al hombre y se arrastra a la mujer.* (Win the man and the woman is dragged along behind.)
2. If the wife accepts first, the husband seldom follows.
3. Evangelical young men who marry non-Evangelical girls almost always win the wife within two years ... Evangelical girls who marry non-Evangelical young men also sometimes win the man, either during courtship or shortly after marriage. In a probable majority of such cases, however, she does not win him.
4. Elderly parents of a new convert seldom accept the new faith.
5. Children of a new convert, who live at home, almost always accept the faith of the parent. Married children of a new convert and some working away from home seldom do (1968:139).

The A. R. P. Church has won entire families, but in many cases there has been a failure to follow out the linkage of kinships which promises a real response. In the rural areas where many of the people are related, it would seem valuable to discover how the family ties have been taken advantage of and how they have not.

Not only must the family connections be taken into consideration, but in both city and country the social structure is an important factor in the growth of the Church. Eugene A. Nida has given a graph of Latin American social structure which is typical of Mexico. See Plate 15.

The upper class of Mexican society, as is true in other Latin American countries, occupies a very small percentage of the entire populace, approximately three per cent. This class is divided into the upper group of the aristocrats, the true elite of the society and the lower group who have only recently acquired wealth and prestige. The middle class has approximately

PLATE 15

THE STRUCTURE OF MEXICAN SOCIETY

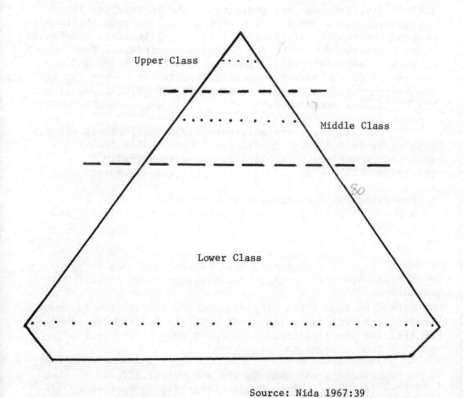

Source: Nida 1967:39

seventeen per cent of the population. Some have been able to move up into this class due to the emphasis on education and the goal of the government to make schooling available for the masses. Most young people in Mexico today have an opportunity to attend the six years of primary school and many elect to continue their education, completing secondary school and often some professional course. This enables them to better themselves in society by securing better jobs. The upper group of this class includes the doctors, lawyers, professors, politicians, engineers and businessmen. In the bottom half we find other white-collar workers such as clerks, bookkeepers, small businessmen, teachers and ministers. The lower class is by far the largest segment of the population with some eighty per cent of the people falling into that classification. The upper lower class includes the less prosperous tradesmen, factory workers, independent small farmers, domestic workers and day laborers. At the very bottom of the social scale are the extremely poor seasonal workers, the indigent share-croppers and the habitually unemployed.

Those within the different social groupings tend to participate together in social functions. They usually look for a mate from their own class and they have essentially the same interests and look at matters with the same viewpoint.

Protestantism has traditionally appealed to the lower class. As Barnett in writing of the acceptance or rejection of new ideas says:

> An individual will not accept a novelty unless in his opinion it satisfies a want better than some existing means at his disposal (1953:378).

He gives the four types of persons who are most open to acceptance of innovations as the dissident, the indifferent, the resentful and the disaffected. Barnett says of the work of William Duncan among the Tsimshian:

> Many others who came to him were disillusioned or frustrated because they found themselves confronted by dilemnas which made any new way of life attractive as an avenue of escape (1953:405).

Thus for these and other reasons, those of the lower class have been more responsive to the Gospel. They recognize more than any others that they are the weak and heavy laden and the invitation of Jesus evokes a response.

Eugene Nida feels that Protestants have done well in

working with this group of people because the future lies with
the masses. Many of those who are today reshaping Latin life
have come primarily from the upper lower class and the lower
middle class. Some feel that Protestantism would be in a
stronger position today if the Church could point to a more
extensive achievement in the really backward and remoter rural
districts.

The A. R. P. Church has appealed to the masses and those who
have come into the fellowship through the years have been from
that portion of the populace. However, particularly in the
urban areas the membership of our churches presents a cross
section of social groups. Can this have been responsible for
some of the slow growth? Have we concentrated too much on
individuals and not enough on groups?

> More and more we must dream in terms of winning groups,
> not merely individuals ... Experience shows that it is
> much better if an entire natural group--a family, a
> village, a caste, a tribe--can come rapidly into the
> faith (McGavran 1968:125).

Too, those who come into the Church tend to move up the
social scale and our Mission has encountered the problem of

> the planting of small clusters of non-growing congre-
> gations which strive to be middle-class and form tiny
> enclaves in a huge population (McGavran 1970:264).

Lift which comes through educational, medical and economical
opportunities profferred by the missionary is a part of the
picture, but it must not outweigh the redemption which is
essential to church growth. There must be a proper balance
between the two. Nida says concerning the lift which evangelicals find in their association with the Church:

> However, this same upward mobility tends to separate
> those concerned from the very groups out of which they
> have come (1960:105).

It becomes difficult for the Mexican who has moved up out of
his social class to reach down and effectively communicate
with the lower classes. He does not wish to endanger his new
status. We have discovered this in our Mission as young people
have left their country villages to study, and on their return
either locate in a large city or fail to speak with meaning to
those who have remained in the lower level.

Moreover, the Protestant church has had from the

strictly indigent, drifting classes few who could provide
leadership to reach out to bring in other persons of the
same group (Nida 1960:107).

This is a problem confronted by missions everywhere and one
which in particular is present on the A. R. P. field. It is a
crucial one. It is one which must be solved by the "old line"
denominations if the growth which we desire is to be attained.

> In the battle between the classes and the masses, the
> masses are going to win. The future belongs to the
> common man. The Churches and their missions must not be,
> or even appear to be, on the side of the already defeated
> upper classes. Jesus Christ is the champion of the poor
> oppressed ... Blessed are the poor for theirs is the
> Kingdom of Heaven (McGavran 1962:40).

Marriage Customs

The marriage customs in Mexico have had a tremendous influence on the growth of the Church. Anyone to be baptized and become a communing member of the Mexican A. R. P. Church must be
legally married and not living under common-law bounds. For
a marriage to be legal, it must be performed by a civil authority for which a small fee of some four dollars is charged.
Christians may later be married in a church ceremony if they
desire, but the civil service comes first. However, some
Latins feel no necessity to be tied by legal procedure.

> Although free unions constituted approximately 20 per
> cent of all marriages in the nation according to the 1950
> census, the children of such marriages are considered to
> be illegitimate by church and civil law. Nevertheless,
> on the local community level, both urban and rural,
> these marriages are socially acceptable. In terms of
> lower class standards, only children who have not been
> recognized or supported by their fathers are considered
> illegitimate (Lewis 1959:17).

This situation is prevalent in all parts of the country, but
is more common in the rural areas. If a man, a woman or both
accept Christ and desire to be baptized and be united with the
Church, they are refused if they are living together in a
common law marriage. Sometimes they have been "wed" for as long
as twenty years and have four or more children. However, they
do not wish to be legally married because of the money involved,
the finality of the marriage document or some other reason.
A member of a lower class family on whom Oscar Lewis did an

extensive study stated quite simply when asked:

> I had never thought of going through a civil or church
> wedding, it simply never occurred to me, and that is true
> of most of the men and women I know (Lewis 1961:58).

This has kept people out of our Church and in all probability
accounts for much of the slow growth in the rural sections. Ob-
viously it is a problem with other Churches as well as many have
voiced their concern. One missionary in Latin America appealed
to his mission board and gained permission to baptize those
who came in repentance and faith in spite of their marital status. The new policy he was instituting was not one of moral
laxity. Far from it. He says:

> Many are astounded, erroneously concluding that we have
> "lowered the standards." ... It is not simply because we
> now baptize all truly repentant believers. It is rather,
> if I have judged correctly, that we - like Peter - give a
> positive invitation: "Repent and be baptized every one
> of you..."Yesterday, for example, eight new believers sat
> as a group in a small village learning that they should
> now be baptized (McGavran 1969b: 32).

He reported that the effect of this policy on church growth had
been tremendous. Churches were multiplying like never before,
but only in those areas where the workers accepted the new
policy. How our Church will treat the same problem is unknown.
A reinvestigation and rethinking of the whole situation is
necessary.

Sympathizers

The total evangelical community includes not only the communicant membership, but the children of believers and a rather
large group of unbaptized believers who attend services. The
latter, called sympathizers, form a big part of the total
community of the A. R. P. Church. These "friends of the Gospel"
attend services, read the Bible, participate in many of the
activities of the Church and believe in Christ, yet for one
reason or another do not unite with the body of believers.
Some in this category may be "almost persuaded." Others cannot
give up a certain way of life in compliance with the high moral
standards set by the Protestant faith which takes a definite
stand against drink, tobacco and concubinage. Some few do not
unite with the Church because of small doctrinal problems, such
as the baptism of children. Others are hindered by pre-conver-
sion marital entanglements.

Satisfied with the blessings received and feeling no concrete, binding reponsibilities, the sympathizers are content to "ride along" for many years. They feel that for the present it is enough to read the Bible and believe in Christ and we, as a Church and a Mission, have not challenged that opinion. Some remain in this nebulous position for more than five years. Statistics from our field indicate that in 1970 we have approximately one thousand sympathizers (remember these are adults!) with only a total membership of two thousand three hundred eighty-nine. Certainly there is need for concern here and active steps should be taken to bring these into the fold.

Problems of Communication

In order for redemption to take place, and hence, church growth, there must be communication of the Gospel. The missionary, as a potential church planter, does not always find this task simple for as Nida has said:

> People differ greatly in their capacities to verbalize, even in their own mother tongue, and there is an even greater problem when they try to communicate in a foreign language (1960:159).

Also in order to communicate, he must identify himself with the people. This does not mean mere imitation of the Mexican way of life, but in a much broader sense a true participation with the national in his own culture. This ability to think and feel like someone of another culture is not easily acquired and for that reason the effectiveness of those who have been able to stay on the field for only one, two or three years was not fully realized.

The missionary must understand the goals, objectives and purposes of the people with whom he works. Although he may not agree with them, he should know why they do certain things. And basic to all communication and acculturation is a genuine love for the national.

This problem of communication has undoubtedly bothered each of our missionaries to some extent or other and has played a part in the slowness of the growth of the Church. There are many examples of the difficulties of communication in the common expressions used in the proclamation of the Gospel.

> It might be assumed that one could translate literally into Spanish the expression 'to receive Christ,' but in Spanish *recibir a Cristo* does not mean to the average

Roman Catholic what it means to the Protestant missionary.
Rather than carrying the sense of personal commitment to
Jesus Christ, it more often than not means 'to receive the
wafer of the eucharist' (Nida 1960:72).

The problem of communication does not rest entirely with the
missionary, however. Most of our work has been in the rural
areas, and yet the majority of the ordained ministers reside in
the cities. As they have several preaching points under their
supervision and must periodically make visits to baptize new
believers, officiate at the Lord's Supper or bring a series of
special messages, these men are often guilty of talking over the
heads of their "poor country cousins."

Another problem lies with the layworkers themselves who live
in the rural villages and ranches. They find that the dialect
varies from region to region and state to state and that often
it is not easy to converse freely. Having had little education
and little training in how to present the Gospel, their preparation for Sunday is often lackadaisical and therefore their
methods are uninviting. The work of the Holy Spirit has been the
deciding factor in the success that many of these consecrated
Christians have had. Their lack of training and resulting lack
of ability to communicate their beliefs have proven a deterrent
to the growth of the Church.

Diaconisas, young ladies trained in Christian education, have
been used in many parts of our work in Mexico. Although they
have excellent preparation, there is one serious cultural draw-
back in their service as "ministers" to the rural congregations.
It is not acceptable socially for them to concentrate on winning
the men. The result, therefore, is a congregation of women and
children, which though not bad, does not aid the ultimate goal
of winning an entire family and community. Here again the problem of communication is present.

Folk Beliefs

Certain folk beliefs have been the enemy of the Gospel in
many sections. Oscar Lewis made a study of a village in Mexico
which has given a picture of life by the typical Mexican peasant. He writes that "saints are seen as intermediaries between
God and man: (Lewis 1960:86). Protestants have found that it
is easier to challenge any belief of the Roman Catholic Church
other than that concerning the Virgin Mary.

The reason, of course, is that the Virgin Mary is not
merely a religious symbol, but a social one as well, and
as such a focus of Latin life (Nida 1960:130).

Other customs have to do with illness. Peasant women tie
various herbs around the necks of their babies to ward off sickness. The extremes of hot and cold are to be avoided in suc-
cession. A woman who has been ironing could not be expected to
attend a church service, because the necessary bath would be
cold and would be bad for her. New mothers are supposed to
remain relatively inactive until forty days have passed. Many
folk beliefs are connected with death. Often the deceased's
favorite food is prepared and placed on his grave on the Day of
the Dead for him to eat. In general, such folk beliefs, have
raised a barrier to the communication of the Gospel and this,
fostered by the illiteracy among the adult rural population
has slowed the extension of the Church in those areas.

Work in Slow Growth Areas

A final obstacle to church growth in the A. R. P. field is
the fact that part of our ministry is being carried on in areas
where the potential for growth is slight. In *Church Growth in
Mexico*, Dr. McGavran has described such areas. One is that of
the conservative cities, including Guadalajara, Guanajuato,
Aguascalientes, Durango and San Luis Potosi. "For historic,
geographic, social, and political reasons these have shown
themselves unresponsive to the Gospel" (McGavran 1963:37). In
San Luis Potosí where we have had an organized church for a
number of years there are still only thirty-five members. Although enthusiasm seems to be picking up, the outlook for the
future in that city is not bright.

Other sections are the small towns, where a large Roman
Catholic Church dominates the scene, the Roman *ranchos* where
sentiment is still largely pro-Catholic and the revolutionary
ranches and *ejidos* where family pressures and spiritual in-
difference often prevent wide acceptance of the faith. Many
of the towns, *ejidos* and ranches where the A. R. P. Church has
planted congregations could fall into one of these categories.
I do not advocate abandoning these congregations. By no means!
We should, however, occupy these areas lightly until a response
is indicated and concentrate on the more winnable places.

The problem then is one of finding the field where the cotton is ready to be picked. As a Southern lad who used to earn
money for the fair by picking cotton, I can well remember that
an important factor to success was the selection of a good
field. In surveying the list of places where there are A. R. P.
congregations (See Appendix A) it can be noted by the number
of members and community in each, just which sections have
shown to be responsive and which have not.

Nida has typified the patterns of reaction to the communication of the Christian faith in the following way:

> (1) Almost complete rejection, (2) indifference, (3) slow but steady acceptance by a small minority, (4) rapid acceptance by a fast growing group, and (5) acceptance by one group and strong resistance or fanatical opposition by another (1960:149).

It is of utmost importance then that we evaluate the area and the response which the Church has met there, asking ourselves if the funds, personnel and effort invested are bringing the desired results. Two examples will illustrate our concern.

A PICTURE OF TWO RURAL CONGREGATIONS

Cerrito de la Cruz

This ranch with a population of approximately one thousand offers a concrete example of the slow growth experienced in many similar locations. Situated near the town of Rayon, San Luis Potosi, Cerrito de la Cruz has been evangelized by the A.R.P. Mission. However, after ten years of Christian testimony by lay preachers on a weekly basis and quarterly visits by ministers of the A. R. P. Synod of Mexico, only ten members are on the roll. Thirty sympathizers and children attend the services giving a total community of forty persons.

A ministry was first begun there in 1959 when David Dorado found a few sympathizers. In such a manner has much of our church planting been done. Shortly thereafter, two young girls took charge of the new station, going each Sunday to hold church school classes in the home of a sympathizer. In 1965 a seminary student, Moises Pacheco, was given the responsibility of the preaching point. The following year a lay couple, Sr. Ramon Alvarado and his wife, Sra. Eustolia Juarez de Alvarado, were placed in Rayon with instructions to visit Cerrito de la Cruz and carry on the ministry there. This couple is still in charge of the field at the present time.

No lay worker has ever lived in Cerrito de la Cruz. For ten years services have been held in a home. The Mission has given $40 for the right to use a lot in the village and another $40 to build a small shed for a Sunday School. On their weekly visits the lay workers carry bricks to be used in constructing a chapel. During the past year four adults were received as communing members and at the present time three women seek

baptism. One, however, is living in common-law wedlock and must
be married legally before being received into the church. The
main group of interested persons is from five to seventeen years
in age.

This congregation probably will never be numerous nor can
it alone employ a lay preacher. In combination with
other villages it could do so. The prospect of a local
farmer becoming a congregational leader is at present
nebulous (Halliday 1969-1970: Private correspondance).

Canada Grande

Also located in the state of San Luis Potosi, Canada Grande
has an approximate population of 1,200. It is halfway between
the capital of the state where there is a small A. R. P.
Church and Rioverde, the site of a larger church and our denominational seminary. Canada Grande is the chief of eight
villages in the Plain of Santa Catarina.

When roads were opened making the village accesible by bus,
the A. R. P. Mission sent Sr. Simon Hernandez, a veteran lay
worker in to survey the prospects. He was helped by Sr. Guadalupe Hernandez, a blind colporteur, who cruised the region
where he was already known, selling Bibles. Next a young lady
was sent into the area. She found friends, taught Sunday
School and gave classes in dress making to the young women of
the village. She was followed by Sra. Angela Garcia de Lopez
who conducted regular worship services and in addition gave
some classes in first aid. Two young men, sons of the common-
law wife of a local farmer-businessman were baptized. At the
present there are three communicants and a community of forty
children and sympathizers.

In 1961, when a seminary student was sent out to preach at
Canada Grande on week ends, his wife who was a nurse laid the
foundation for what was to be the J. L. Pressly Dispensary
(See Chapter IV).

The ministry was begun in the patio of a prominent *ejida-
tario,* Sr. Bernadino Maya. He is a nephew of the blind colporteur who was one of the first to sow the seed of the Gospel. However, although he and his family are openly friendly
to the Gospel they have not yet made a decision to follow
Jesus Christ.

Interest is being generated now by a group of sympathizers
to construct a chapel. Services have been held in the building

used for the Dispensary. Many are praying that those already
interested and others might commit themselves completely to
Christ. Yet in spite of the years invested there and the lift
given through the medical mission work, the harvest has been
slim. It seems as if the time for reaping has not come.

Similar stories can be found in the lives of congregations
scattered throughout our denomination, some in San Luis Potosi,
some in Tamaulipas and others in Vera Cruz. In looking at
these discouraging aspects in the growth of the Church, we must
evaluate our present situation.

What plantings do I have near me? Which are ripest? Where
is the unharvested crop likely to rot in the field? Where
do the winds blow as to assist winnowing? Which are the
unripe plantings where the task is that of watching? ...
It is essential to discern each separate community and its
degree of readiness (McGavran 1966:44).

4

Contemporary Institutional
Contributions to Church Growth

INTRODUCTION

The Associate Reformed Presbyterian Mission has engaged in
institutional work in Mexico since the very early years of
missionary endeavor there. The emphasis placed on this phase
of the program is certainly no different from that of other
"old line" denominations with an established national Church.
The importance we have given to it has perhaps been less than
that by some groups and more than by others.

At the present time the Mission is involved in three types
of institutional work: educational, which includes a seminary,
two dormitories for primary school children and scholarship aid
in the field of higher education; literary, in the form of a
book store; and medical, with a twenty-five bed clinic and a
small dispensary. All of the missionaries on the field work
with these institutions as well as in the evangelistic ministry.
There is no one institution, with the exception of the clinic,
which requires the missionary's full time.

Plate 16 indicates the percentage of the total budget spent
in these areas. The following presentation will give some idea
of the depth of our involvement in this field and the value that
it has in the overall picture of the Church.

EDUCATIONAL WORK

The Seminary

A trained leadership is important to the growth of any

PLATE 16

DISTRIBUTION OF THE BUDGET OF THE
ASSOCIATE REFORMED PRESBYTERIAN MISSION IN MEXICO
1971

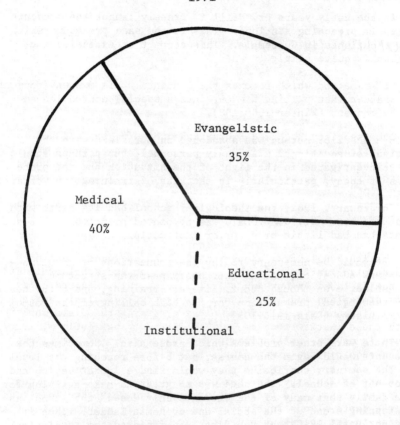

Evangelistic

35%

Medical

40%

Educational

25%

Institutional

Source: Associate Reformed Presbyterian Mission 1969

Church. McGavran in writing of the preparation of the ministry has said:

> We are called to create a ministry which will keep growing Churches growing and start non-growing Churches on the road of great growth (1966:142).

Since the beginning of the mission work of the A. R. P. Church in Mexico there has been some type of training.

In the early years Dr. Neill E. Pressly taught the students at their preaching stations. This is the same procedure which now flourishes in Guatemala. This concept of extension education is quite simply

> that method which reaches the student in his own environment rather than pulling him out into a special controlled environment (Winter 1969:153).

This concept or method was abandoned on our field with the arrival of additional missionary personnel, but perhaps should be reinvestigated in the light of the situation and the problems of today, particularly in the area of training lay workers.

In January, 1901, the theological school had its birth with two students. Dr. J. G. Dale was appointed principal. The students had had little or no prior instruction.

> It would be necessary to lay the foundations of an elementary education, and on this basis rear the structure of a solid, even though short, literary training, and a further theological preparation for the high calling of the gospel ministry (Dale 1910:163).

There were other problems which arose also. Sometimes the students would begin the course, but before reaching the level of the seminary curriculum they would find a lucrative job and drop out of school. The need was so great to make a living for the family that many of the students only "used" the school as a stepping stone up the social and economic ladder. Thus it was not until 1910 that the first man finished the theological school in Rioverde, S. L. P.

This first institution was known as *The Preparatory and Theological School.* From 1906-1913 it was called *The Rio Verde Bible School.* From this period came four men trained for the ministry. With the Revolution came a standstill in the theological training of the nationals as well as in all other phases of the mission work. When Dr. Dale was able to return

to the field in 1919, he located in Tampico and during a ten
year stay there was able to train three ministers and two colporteurs. Once again the principle of training was more closely
akin to the idea of extension education.

From 1933-1960, the school was named *The Rio Verde Bible
Institute* with Dr. W. C. Halliday at the helm. Now that the
institution is run jointly by the Mission and the Mexican A.R.P.
Synod it is known as the *Seminario Teologico Presbiteriano
Asociado Reformado*. It is a small seminary with few students,
few buildings, few professors and a limited range of studies.
Dr. Halliday continues to serve as the director and is a member of the administrative board which includes nationals as
well.

There have been and still are many problems in the training
of the ministry. The students come from different local situations and with varying scholastic backgrounds. Most, at
least until ten years ago, had little or no secular schooling,
a fact which necessitated general education before they could
be taught seminary subjects. Many of the students could not
endure the many years needed to undergo such a pretheological
course and therefore many dropped out.

Since 1961 all students have been required to hold an A. B.
degree in order to enter the seminary. The percentage of
those holding such a degree in Mexico is small, and smaller
still the number of church members having reached that level
of schooling. When we consider the number of those "qualified"
who feel called to enter the ministry, it becomes evident why
so few are in the seminary.

The Presbyterian Church has always been noted for its concentration on an educated ministry. Certainly its importance
to the Church cannot be denied, but as has been stated:

> There is no surer way to choke church growth than to cre-
> ate a highly educated one-level ministry which by training
> is out of tune with the rank and file of new members and
> will not work for what the new churches pay (McGavran 1966:
> 137).

Also the spiritual qualifications of the candidates for the
ministry cannot be overlooked. Perhaps in emphasizing the educational we are bypassing some of our spiritually qualified
natural leaders. There must be a balance. We must train men
in their own culture who are atuned to the needs of the common
people. The spiritual aspect should be the essential with
scholarship also adhered to.

Periodically the seminary has offered classes for the paid
lay workers who in reality form the bulk of the preaching force
in our mission field. Short institutes have been conducted for
their benefit from four days to one month in length. Out station classes in Christian education have also been a part of
the seminary program. The possibilities of such programs are
great and deserve to be considered in view of what has happened
in theological education in Latin America in the past decade.

The story of the seminary is not all one of problems by any
means. One of the national ministers declared: "The seminary
has progressed notably" (Lopez 1970: Letter to Author). Men
trained there are making a magnificent contribution to the
ministry of the Church.

As the A. R. P. Seminary looks to the future several questions
arise. Will the A. R. P. Synod be able to finance the seminary
and furnish the personnel? Classes are held in the classrooms
of the local church. Does its size limit the training? Is it
in the best location? What are the possibilities for enlarging
the field of training?

To complete the picture of the seminary we give a list of
those who have served as professors recently or who are serving
at the present time.

> W. C. Halliday, B.D., S.T.B., Th. M., D.D., President and
> Dean.
> Maurilio Lopez, Grad. Sem. P.A.R., with a year of study in
> the Seminary at Matanzas, Cuba, Pre-Castro. Secretary of
> Consejo.
> Patrick G. Covone, B.D. (U.S.A.).
> Ruben Castaneda, Grad. Sem. P.A.R., with a year of study in
> Union Seminary at Rio Piedras, Puerto Rico.
> Eufrasio Perez L., Grad. Centro Unido Evangelico, Mexico
> City with one semester in Puerto Rico.
> Amador Pesina G., Grad. Seminary P.A.R. with a year of
> study at Baptist Seminary, Los Angeles.
> Ramon O. Reyes, Grad. of A.R.P. Seminary at Tampico, 1926.
> Jose Rodriguez S., Grad. of Centro Unido Evangelico of
> Mexico City.
> Robert A. Whitesides, B.D., Th. M.
> Robert L. Brawley, B.D. (Halliday 1969-1970: Private
> correspondence).

Erskine Theological Seminary

The institution corresponding to our seminary in Mexico is

the Erskine Theological Seminary supported by the A. R. P. Church
in the United States. How has this school contributed to church
growth in Mexico? The most significant contribution has been in
the preparation of personnel for the field. Of the male missionaries on the field at this writing, five have received their
theological education at the Erskine Seminary and the remaining
two are laymen (Rodriguez and Mitchell).

Such statistics are not new, for in looking over the roster
of those who have served on the field, we find that the majority
of the male missionaries are graduates of Erskine Theological
Seminary. The training received is theologically sound, however because of the high percentage of students preparing for
the ministry in the United States, the curriculum is geared to
their needs.

Subjects such as cultural anthropology, mission theory and
church structure in our foreign mission fields are greatly
needed by those who go into the missionary service. These should
be included in the seminary curriculum. More emphasis should
be placed on the world mission of the Church, which includes
our own country. Such courses, adjusted to give not only theory
but the practical aspects of the ministry, would be invaluable
and could revolutionize the Church.

The Primary School

In the early years of our mission endeavor in Mexico, there
was a great thrust in the field of education, particularly on
the primary school level as the missionaries realized they were
ministering to a people that was largely illiterate. Ramon
Eduardo Ruiz paints the picture of those years in his book
Mexico: The Challenge of Poverty and Illiteracy:

> During the banner year of 1910 the Diaz regime spent less
> than 7 per cent of its income on education. Nearly 85 per
> cent of the population was illiterate; the percentage in
> rural areas soared beyond this. Hundreds of villages had
> no one able to read and write. Only 5 per cent of the
> population was in school, one fourth of Mexico's school
> children (1963:8).

The mission supported schools opened doors of previously closed
homes and hearts to the Gospel. However, with new laws it became no longer prudent nor legal for the Mission to finance and
work in schools. For that reason, the A. R. P. Church in Mexico
today has only one primary school with which it is connected.

This is *Colegio Juarez* (literally the College of Juarez) located in Ciudad Valles, S. L. P. It is a private institution
with kindergarten through grade six. This primary school is
established according to the Mexican laws and is operated by
nationals. Our resident missionaries, Pat and Imogene Covone,
do participate on the board of directors when elected, but
officially neither the Church nor the Mission has a direct hand
in the school. The principal, Jesus Alfaro, and all the teachers
are Protestants. The members of the board of directors are
also Protestant with the majority being members of the A. R. P.
Church. The students represent all classes in Ciudad Valles
and the surrounding areas,but most would be classified from the
upper lower class. The Mission financially supports about
thirty students each year in Colegio Juarez. These students
live in dormitories supported and operated by the Mission, Janie
Love Home for Girls and Sara Flores Home for Boys. In most
cases the students are children of church members.

With education so much a part of our life in the United
States, it is difficult to realize that in Mexico, in spite of
the tremendous emphasis which recent presidents have placed on
providing schooling for all, there are still rural areas where
there is no school or, at the most, only three grades. If a
young person from this situation wants a formal education he
must go to one of the larger towns or cities. Therefore he
leaves home at eight, nine or ten years of age and goes to live
with a relative, a friend or in a mission dormitory.

The Covones supervise the two dormitories supported by our
Mission. A Mexican housemother lives in each to cook and be
a Christian "mother" to the children. The students who are
selected to live in the hostel must be worthy of the honor.
They must come from a village or settlement where there is no
school, they must not have a brother or sister in the school at
the same time and they must be recommended by a pastor, missionary or lay worker. Of course there are exceptions to the rule.
The goal is to give a fair representation to all areas where
the A. R. P. Church has work.

While in the dormitories the boys and girls are presented
with the Gospel through the local church and through the witness of the housemothers and the missionaries. The majority
make a profession of faith while there. Some, in doing so, become second generation Christians and others as first generation Christians can carry the Gospel back to their families for
the first time.

The comprehensive totals in the mission budget for 1971 show
a request for $4,800 for the primary school students, $1,200

for salaries of housemothers and $600 for upkeep of the build-
ings. It is the feeling of the author that the support of this
institution does have a positive effect on the growth of our
Church, both in the city where it is located and in the pro-
vinces from where the dormitory students come.

Higher Education

   The A. R. P. Mission in Mexico supports no schools or dormitories for students on the secondary and professional levels.
Scholarship funds are available, however, for qualified young
men and women. In the early years of the mission endeavor such
institutions were a part of the scene. Much has already been
mentioned about these in early chapters. The higher education
for young ladies was begun by Mrs. John Edwards through the
orphanage she established in Rioverde, S. L. P. Through the
years others have added to this ministry. At the present Mrs.
W. C. Halliday is in charge of the scholarships given to young
ladies and Dr. Halliday for those given to young men.

   The recipients of these scholarships come primarily from our
Christian community. The selection is made from those students
who show the best prospects, grades and personality and who
evidence the greatest possibilities for later effectiveness in
the work of the Church. All are from needy families. Whenever
the parents are able partially to support their son or daughter
in school, such an arrangement is worked out. It is felt that
this system of partial subsidy is most effective because the
funds can be stretched to help more students, and the family
gains a sense of responsibility and accomplishment. Such a
policy has been in effect in our Mission since 1941. Students,
selected by the Hallidays, have come from all over the Synod.
They have attended different schools and been engaged in
various courses of study. The time and effort involved in
selecting, counselling and guiding these young people is tremendous.

   Many of the secondary students are able to attend school in
their home town with the aid of a scholarship. This is ideal
as it does not take them out of their familiar surroundings
nor out of the bounds of our Church. Others, coming from
small ranches and villages where no such facilities are available, must live in a Christian hostel in another town. There,
although in a Christian atmosphere, they are away from their
families and the A.R.P. Church.

   The professional students, almost without exception, must
leave their homes to attain the training they desire. Since

1941, one hundred eighty-two young ladies have received scholarship aid from the Mission in preparing for life service. They
have studied dressmaking, commercial courses, church music,
Christian education, nurses'training, education (teacher training in a normal school) and practical nursing courses. A like
number of young men have also been helped doing preparatory
school work and studying medicine, law, agronomy and such courses.

Mrs. Halliday in speaking of the value of participating in
such an educational project has written:

> Without exception, perhaps, the special training given
> these young ladies (and men) has resulted in a raising of
> the level in which their families lived. Not all of these
> are strong church members at present - we wish this were
> true, but quite a few of them are taking their places in
> their homes and in the church and in society, giving a
> good testimony for Christ (1969: Letter to author).

Many of these students have become teachers in Colegio Juarez
and other schools, nurses in the Neill E. Pressly Clinic, doctors
serving in our clinic, ministers for our denomination, directors
of Christian education working in the rural mission stations and
secretaries for the clinic and bookstore. A large number are
active members of our Church providing a trained young leadership.

But how much has this affected the growth of the Church.
Senorita Maria Cleofas Castillo Alvarez (now Sra. Cleofas C. de
Lopez) received a mission scholarship to attend secondary
school. She came into the Church with her entire family (a type
of people movement). The father, who was a heavy drinker, gave
up this vice; both father and mother are still active members
of the church. Mrs. Castillo is treasurer of the woman's society
and Mr. Castillo is an elder. After finishing high school,
Cleofas went to nursing school at the Presbyterian U. S. hospital
in Morelia, Michoacan, again on a mission scholarship, and on
graduation served as head nurse for the N. E. Pressly Clinic for
seven years until her marriage in 1968. Another member of the
family, Petra, also studied nursing on a mission scholarship and
has worked in the clinic. Cleofas and Petra have sent another
sister to normal school, one to nursing school and a brother to
engineering school. The strong family ties here can be noted,
as with help to one girl, a chain reaction was begun which resulted in an entire family's coming into the Church and the
education of all the younger members.

Other cases are similar. Perhaps the direct result on church
growth has not been as evident in all situations since some have
been church members before receiving help with their education,

yet their contributions to the life and leadership of the Church
have been notable. A director of Christian education married her
childhood sweetheart, a non-Christian. After ten years and six
children he was converted and asked for baptism. It is his
tithe which is providing most of the money to construct a
church in the state capital. Four young ladies, studying in
that city, gave up their holiday to help pour a concrete floor
in the church under construction.

The proposed budget for 1971 shows a comprehensive sum of
$11,190 to be used in the field of higher education. It is an
investment in young lives which is hoped will pay off in
leaders for our Church and a growth of the same.

THE GOSPEL BOOKSTORE

The A. R. P. Mission has had a gospel bookstore in Mexico
called the *Libreria Las Buenas Nuevas* (The Good News Bookstore).
At this writing it has just been sold to a chain of Christian
bookstores *La Antorcha, S. A.*   due to the resignation of the
missionaries who have been supervising it. The Mission felt
that it was no longer possible to maintain this institution.

It is very unlikely that accurate information could be found
defining to just what extent the bookstore has aided the development of the emerging Protestant movement in Mexico. However,
there are some concrete, positive factors that do give an insight into the contribution made by this institution.

> For one thing it certainly has served as a supply depot for
> 'ammunition' with which to fight against superstition, ig-
> norance, and prejudice (Whitesides, R. A. 1969: Letter to
> author).

Before March 21, 1955, the date when the bookstore was established, there were colporteurs who distributed the Scriptures
in Mexico. At about this period they were being replaced by
gospel bookstores. In the Tampico area there was no place where
one could buy the Holy Bible, Christian literature or Sunday
School materials. Thus *La Libreria Las Buenas Nuevas* came into
being to meet a felt need. Its conception was inspired and fostered by Robert and Harriett Lou Whitesides who have been in
charge of the bookstore from that time until the present day.

One can hardly imagine a city of 50,000 in the United States
or England without at least one Christian bookstore. Yet until
1955 in the whole area served by our Church - an area of three
states - there was such a vacuum. Our store was one of the first

to be opened outside of Mexico City.

Mr. Whitesides feels that the spiritual life of our church members must have been influenced by both the Scriptures and other Christian literature obtained in this bookstore. By having this storehouse of material available, it has facilitated the work of the minister, the missionary and the layman, and as a direct result, the work of the Church in which they are engaged.

An open Bible has been kept in the window in view of the public eye since the opening of *Las Buenas Nuevas*. Many times people will stop to read the passage, copy it down or call it to the attention of a friend. This has been a silent testimony for the past fifteen years, a fact which in itself could have encouraged some to attend an evangelical church, although not necessarily our particular branch of the Church.

This work has also fostered a close cooperation with other Protestant denominations. The store sells publications from all leading groups. Mr. Whitesides comments:

> When our people have seen Baptist, Methodist, Presbyterian and Nazarene publications for sale in the same place, they naturally have a tendency to recognize as equals and brothers those who may belong to some other Protestant denominations (1969: Letter to author).

At the time the bookstore was organized, there seemed to be an attitude of inferiority within the Protestant ranks. In order to be accepted socially in our section of Mexico, one had to be a Catholic. A Protestant was considered a social outcast. It was not unusual to see on the doors of many homes in Tampico and the surrounding towns a printed notice that said something like this: "This is a patriotic, Catholic home and we energetically reject all Protestant and Communistic propaganda" (Whitesides, R. A. 1969: Letter to author). Because of this feeling of antagonism, for years and years most Protestant services were held at night so the general public could not identify those who attended.

The very fact that for a decade and a half we have had a Protestant bookstore in a prominent place offering the Word of God to anyone has given the evangelicals more self respect. Now even Catholic customers purchase Protestant literature for use in their churches. There is a wide variety of literature from which to choose, and the quality of the material printed in Spanish has improved through the years.

Just recently a man was in the store buying several items of

literature for small children. Mr. Whitesides, who was there at
the time, asked if he was a Sunday School teacher. The man re-
plied in the negative and continued to explain:

> Actually, I am not a member of any church. But I am buy-
> ing this for my own child to read to him. I surely don't
> want him to grow up to be a hippie! (Whitesides, R. A. 1969:
> Letter to author).

So it is that we cannot measure the extent of the ministry of
the gospel bookstore for we are dealing with intangibles. We
do believe, however, that this endeavor has been beneficial to
many Christians, not only those who are members of the A. R.
Presbyterian Church. This ministry has made the heavy load a
little lighter, has extended the Kingdom of God a little farther
and has made readily available God's Word at a nominal cost.

MEDICAL WORK

Dr. Neill Erskine Pressly

Today in Mexico there are thousands who are suffering from
lack of medical attention. If this situation exists in our
modern age, we can only imagine what it must have been like
ninety years ago. Undoubtedly Neill E. Pressly looked with com-
passion on those suffering people and felt he could serve God
better by helping alleviate physical pain.

This was to be an "extra" as he had gone to Mexico to do evangelistic work, and he did not lessen his efforts in that area.
Rather, learning medicine from an American doctor in Tampico,
he made it an important adjunct to his witness.

> He served as doctor among the poor of the city; and when
> he made regular visits to the mission centers in northern
> Vera Cruz, he ministered to the bodies of the sick even as
> he ministered to the souls (Kennedy 1951:631).

Dr. Pressly used medicine to help "break the ice" in those difficult early days. He did not establish a clinic since his primary objective was to visit in many areas and plant churches
whenever possible. Thus the first medical mission work of our
Church was an important factor in the growth.

Dr. Katherine Neel Dale

La Doctora, as she was called by the Mexicans, did a

magnificent work as a medical doctor and a soul winner. She labored so hard that some believe she actually worked herself to death. Her first clinic after her arrival on the mission field was in Ciudad del Maiz, S. L. P. Her interest was clear as it was written of her:

> From the very first when Dr. Neel opened her clinic in Ciudad del Maiz she recognized that the supreme and all-determining purpose of her medical ministry was to save souls. All else was secondary (Dale 1943:69).

From Ciudad del Maiz she moved to Rioverde, then Tampico, and finally to Tamanzunchale where she labored among the Indians. Dr. Dale had long hours in her office and then would make house calls. Always she sought a way to witness. National Christians were used to witness to those in the waiting room, and thousands upon thousands of portions of Scripture found their way into Mexican homes and hearts.

The value of the medical mission work and the contribution of Dr. Katherine Dale to church growth is best summed up in these words:

> The Medical Department is more than self-supporting, rendering service to body and soul. So far as men can judge, there is no other department of our missionary activities that is achieving larger spiritual results (Associate Reformed Presbyterian Church 1922:587).

The Neill Erskine Pressly Clinic

From the time of Dr. Dale's death in 1941 until the mid 1950's the A. R. P. Mission had no medical work in Mexico. In the decade previous to her death, Dr. Dale labored among the Indians and this left the area served by our Church without medical work. It is interesting to note that church membership dropped during this period. (See Chapter III.)

In the mid 1950's the missionaries decided that a medical mission work should be reopened and that one of their main objectives was to establish a clinic.

> Without delay we decided that first on our list of needs for the future would surely be a clinic on our field. We had already seen much physical suffering, much of which we had been unable to help. We had felt that many lived in pain needlessly and that others were searching in vain for health as they used the services of untrained and unscrupulous healers (Covone 1967:3).

The goal of the clinic was described as being a strength to the needy with the following three aspects as ramifications of that goal:

> First, the needy find moral strength through the genuine concern shown them in the clinic ... The influence of Christian sympathy and love which encircles the clinic is no doubt the first soothing balm to many and is equally as comforting as medications received later. Secondly, they find physical strength through good care. Thirdly, the needy find spiritual strength through Christ in the clinic (Covone 1961:4).

Ciudad Mante, a growing city on the northernmost end of the mission field, was selected as a site for the clinic. A church had been established there, but no missionary had ever lived in that region.

And so in 1959, the Neill E. Pressly Clinic first opened its doors to the public. Named for our pioneer missionary who had first caught the vision of ministering to the body as well as the soul, the clinic was established for the dual purpose set forth in Luke 10:9 (King James Version): "And heal the sick that are therein and say unto them, the kingdom of God is come nigh unto you.

The clinic work was begun in a small way. A one room house on a side street in Ciudad Mante was rented for the purpose. Equipment was scarce. Dr. David Rodriguez, a Christian from Tampico, was in charge of the two bed institution. A nurse assisted him in the day, but went home at night. It was difficult if not impossible for an American doctor to practice medicine under the existing laws and so no effort was made to secure a missionary doctor. A missionary did come from one hundred miles away on occasion to oversee the work.

The following year a larger house was found on the main street of the city, and the clinic changed locations. The four rooms were equipped with two beds each having a capacity of eight patients. There was also space for an operating room - which served a dual purpose as a delivery room - a kitchen, a small office and several rooms above where Dr. Rodriguez lived with his family. In those early days when the clinic was not yet well known as a Protestant hospital, the townspeople were heard referring to it as the "Elvis Pressly Clinic." When the author arrived in 1962 to become the first resident missionary and fulltime administrator of the clinic, his name was also confused with that of Neill E. Pressly. The Mexican custom of using two last names, the first paternal and the second maternal caused a natural assumption that James Erskine Mitchell must be the grandson of Neill Erskine Pressly.

The medical work thrived and the *Clinica Pressly* became known as a place where good medical attention could be received, often at little or no cost, and also a place where you heard about God's Word and experienced Christian love and concern. A *clinica* in Mexico is a medical institution with less than twenty beds; a *sanatorio* has from twenty-one to fifty beds; and a *hospital*, fifty or more.

The Mission, through a Mexican holding company, had earlier purchased a five acre lot on the edge of the city, and in 1965 the clinic was moved into the first really appropriate building, one which was not rented. The esteem with which the "Protestant intruders" were regarded was noticed by the large number of doctors and city officials who attended the inauguration of the new facilities and the congregation which was present for the dedication service in the local church.

In 1967 the Ethel Young Children's Wing was opened, bringing the capacity to twenty-five beds. A staff of between twenty and twenty-five work there, half of whom are Protestant, with the remaining fifty per cent being divided between "friends" of the Church and Roman Catholics.

The work being done by the clinic in the physical realm is easy to appraise. The devotion of the Christian doctors, the nurses and the entire personnel is attested to by all who go there as patient or visitor. Many have passed through the doors since they were first opened in 1959, and the statistics are impressive.

Yet, it is necessary to ask too, what has been happening in a spiritual way. Are there results to show that the clinic is more than just a clinic? The spiritual statistics are not so easily counted, but positive results have been seen from the personal witness given by the Christians on the staff, the daily devotions, the Bibles and Christian literature which are distributed and the example of God's love in action.

In a medical endeavor such as the clinic, it becomes all too easy to become bogged down in the essential mechanics of running the institution and to leave the spiritual side unattended. When this is done, however, the reason for the medical mission work ceases to exist. As Dr. E. Gettys, chairman of the Board of Foreign Missions stated, his chief concern and that of the Board has always been that the clinic be used in the evangelization of the Mexican people (Gettys 1969a: Interview). The spiritual outreach is by far the most important aspect of the clinic ministry.

Has the clinic had a positive effect on church growth? A man took a Bible from our clinic and later became the first convert in his town where a church was begun. We have seen evidences of fruit being harvested as patients have attended our church, as one of the employees has accepted Christ and as others have returned to their villages with a receptive attitude toward the Gospel. During the past year thirty conversions were reported as a result of the witness of the staff and church members among the patients.

In summary we could conclude by stating that the N. E. Pressly Clinic has produced an abundance of good will and some growth for our church and other evangelical churches in Ciudad Mante and the surrounding country side. The priority of "telling the world" of Christ must be emphasized and every means used to the fullest so that the clinic becomes a real coordinator for church planting. The possibilities are there, but unfortunately they have not been completely developed.

With almost $26,000 asked to be channeled into the clinic work in 1971, we must beware of its becoming "big business."

> In summary, perhaps the test is this: if the school or hospital is helping the Church to grow, it is useful. If not, then its support by funds from overseas, earmarked for the extension of the Church of Jesus Christ, should be seriously questioned (Shearer 1966:206).

Having been more closely associated with the clinic ministry than any other phase of the mission work, the author feels that the impact it can have on the growth of our denomination in the region in which it is located is great. There must be no failure to use the power we have at our finger tips.

Dr. David Rodriguez Enriquez

If God had not called a Christian doctor like David Rodriguez Enriquez, the Neill E. Pressly Clinic could never have been organized. A second generation Christian, dedicated to the church and to his profession, this man is a *maravilla* (marvelous person). When the clinic work was begun, it was he who struggled with the inefficiencies of the equipment and building and who had to meet the ridicule of his professional counterparts. A verse written by the Apostle Paul which David's father had taught him early in life encouraged him to live as a consecrated Christian in a difficult situation. It was Romans 1:16 (R. S. V.):

> For I am not ashamed of the gospel: it is the power of
> God for salvation to every one who has faith, to the Jew
> first and also to the Greek.

God blessed his testimony, and his exemplary Christian life
stands as a witness to many.

Dr. Rodriguez has always been willing to treat every patient,
whether rich or poor - something that many of the national doctors refuse to do. He works long hours and is one of the few
doctors in a city of fifty thousand who will make house calls.
All of this, plus his verbal testimony to his faith, has added
to the image of the A. R. P. Church in the eyes of the population.

Since its beginning Dr. Rodriguez has worked with the N. E.
Pressly Clinic, at times for a salary, and in later years, when
he was also working with the local Social Security Hospital, for
no compensation at all. In June, 1969, Dr. and Mrs. Rodriguez
(Lucia A. de Rodriguez) attended the meeting of the General
Synod of the A. R. P. Church at Bonclarken, North Carolina
offering themselves as missionaries to their own people. Their
appointment was approved by the Board of Foreign Missions and
by the Synod, making them the first national missionaries to
serve on the Mexican field.

Mrs. Rodriguez is taking a nursing course at present so that
she too can contribute to the medical work. This consecrated
couple is an invaluable asset to the medical mission work as
they witness through the clinic, through the church and through
participation in Synod's programs. It is significant that
nationals have played such an important role in the medical work
in the past decade and that they continue to do so. We feel
that this is a healthy sign and that a good trend has been
started.

Dr. Salathiel Saldana Soto

Salathiel Saldana Soto, M. D. received his medical training
with the help of a scholarship from the A. R. P. Mission. After
completing his studies he worked in the Pressly Clinic for a
short while. At present he is a member of the staff of the
Social Security Hospital in Ciudad Valles, S. L. P. where he
specializes in surgery.

Although he does not serve in an official capacity in the

medical mission work, Dr. Saldana makes a significant contribution in that area. He has a particular interest in the Indians who live in the Huasteca Potosina, just thirty miles from his home. Here in the Sierra Madre Oriental mountains the A. R. P. Church has several preaching points, and on his day off it is not uncommon to find this Christian doctor ministering there. The need for medical attention is great, and the need for the Gospel is equally as great. Dr. Saldana goes to give free consultations and medicines, and on most occasions holds a service for the people where he preaches.

Here is a tremendous potential for church growth which we must try to utilize. Dr. Saldana is opening doors and hearts in an area where the possibilities of a people movement are evident. What will this mean to our Mission and our Church in the next decade?

The James L. Pressly Dispensary

When roads were opened up between Rioverde and San Luis Potosi, the A. R. P. Mission sent layworkers into the little village of Canada Grande located almost halfway between these two cities. With a population of 1,200, Canada Grande was the largest of eight villages in that plain.

Various lay workers, paid by the Mission, participated in the proclamation of the Gospel in this new field. In 1961 when Alvaro Jimenez, a seminary student was preaching there on week ends, his wife, a registered nurse, accompanied her husband and began attending the sick. When funds became available the next year a resident nurse took up the infant work. She lived in a Robin Hood house trailor furnished by the Mission and treated patients in a canvas tent. At the end of that year a brick office was built to replace the tent.

In the ensuing years several registered and practical nurses have resided in Canada Grande for varying lengths of time. They attend such cases as knife, club and gunshot wounds, bronchitis, pneumonia, diarrhea and childbirth. There can be no doubt as to the need for medical facilities in this little village, and the dispensary has met that need. Eight hundred dollars come from foreign sources each year to finance this endeavor.

The evangelistic work has not met with equal success. See discussion of this in Chapter III. A serious consideration of continuing a medical ministry in a place which has shown so little response should be made. Perhaps it would bear more fruit in another location.

EVALUATION

In looking at the A. R. P. institutional work as a whole it
is wise to see how others have evaluated the tendency to concentrate on this type of endeavor. McGavran in *Church Growth
in Mexico* wrote of one roadblock to the growth of the Church as
an "insatiable, unrelated institutionalism" (1963:116). He went
on by saying:

> In the process of planting churches, many Christian
> missions build up large institutions, begun for all kinds
> of good reasons, to do all kinds of good deeds. These
> institutions help the public, help the younger Church,
> are indirectly evangelistic, give the Evangelical cause
> prestige - and they gradually use up larger and larger
> proportions of missionaries, budgets, nationals and
> attention. They are insatiable ... The missionaries want
> them, the nationals want them, the boards want them, and
> the sending Churches love them. They appear to be an
> absolutely essential part of Christian mission. They
> divert a very large proportion of mission resources (cash
> and men) to excellent work which has only a slight connec-
> tion with reconciling men to God (1963:116).

Some of the dangers to avoid in institutionalism should be
spotlighted. They include such things as difficult requirements to maintain in the areas of finances and personnel, the
problem of spiritual surveillance, the fact that "super-nationals"
are created, the inability to produce Christian leaders in many
cases, the tendency for the institutions to become top heavy and
their failure to help build up the Church in proportion to the
investments in them.

Without doubt some portions of the institutional work supported by our Mission and the national Church fall in the direct
line of fire of these comments. Other areas of involvement are
both necessary and worthwhile. It is imperative that as the
Mission looks to the future of the national Church that every
effort be made to continually evaluate both the degree and use-
fulness of the institutions and employ those which contribute
most to a strong, growing denomination.

Much might be accomplished if the staff of all our institutions were to study church planting evangelism and devote eight
hours a week (or another block of time) to it. The field of
their evangelistic labors should not be primarily their patients,
ex-patients, school children or parents of school children.
Rather the staff should undertake regular planned church planting in populations considered to be responsive, usually where

one or two baptized believers are to be found. In short each staff should be planting and nurturing a dozen house churches located within an hour or so of the institution.

5

Direct Contributions

to Church Growth

THE ROLE OF THE MISSIONARY

The missionary must be a man of dedication who will consider himself expendable. He must be willing to keep himself mobile and sufficiently flexible so that his program
and plans can be guided by the Spirit of God. He must
not think of himself or his ministry in terms of building his own career, but in terms of giving himself in
order that churches may result (McGavran 1965b:34).

Supposedly everyone has an idea of what the missionary does.
But is this idea mere supposition or is it fact? In this analysis of the role of the missionary we shall look briefly into the
lives and service of those first servants sent out by the
Associate Reformed Presbyterian Board to Mexico and then with
more detail at those who are on the field at the present time.
Drawing from our practical missionary experience in working with
them, we will seek to find some guidelines for the work today
with particular reference to what the missionary can and should
do.

Plate 17 depicts each individual missionary indicating the
length of service. Notice the long period of service of the
pioneer missionaries (39 years). Dr. and Mrs. N. E. Pressly
were the only representatives on the field during the main part
of the Mexican Revolution. The break in the lines of service
indicates that all the other missionary personnel left the field
in 1913 and only two returned in 1916. Look at the long periods
of service near the top of the graph, the short periods near the
middle and then beginning with the Hallidays (1926) the longer

PLATE 17

ASSOCIATE REFORMED PRESBYTERIAN MISSIONARIES IN MEXICO: LENGTH OF SERVICE

1879-1969

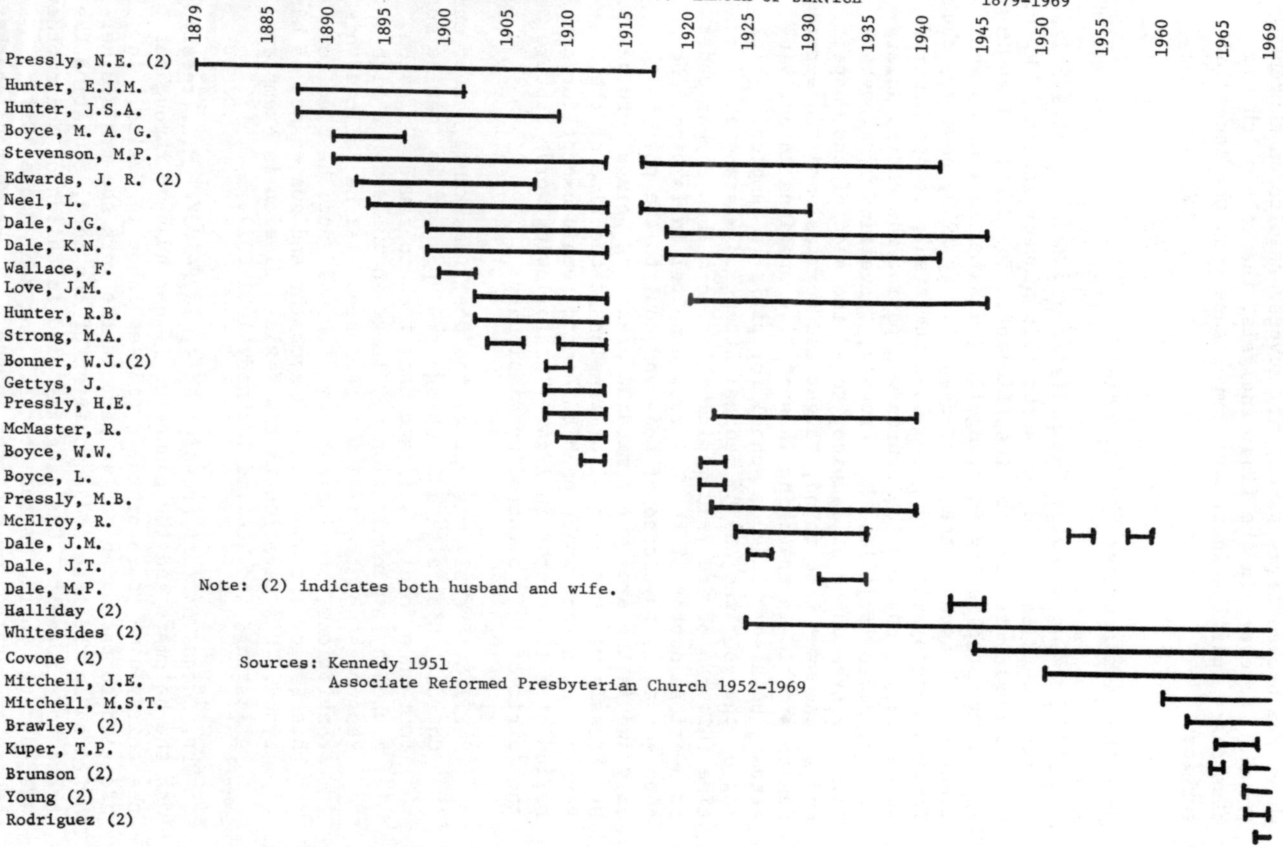

1879 1885 1890 1895 1900 1905 1910 1915 1920 1925 1930 1935 1940 1945 1950 1955 1960 1965 1969

Pressly, N.E. (2)
Hunter, E.J.M.
Hunter, J.S.A.
Boyce, M. A. G.
Stevenson, M.P.
Edwards, J. R. (2)
Neel, L.
Dale, J.G.
Dale, K.N.
Wallace, F.
Love, J.M.
Hunter, R.B.
Strong, M.A.
Bonner, W.J.(2)
Gettys, J.
Pressly, H.E.
McMaster, R.
Boyce, W.W.
Boyce, L.
Pressly, M.B.
McElroy, R.
Dale, J.M.
Dale, J.T.
Dale, M.P.
Halliday (2)
Whitesides (2)
Covone (2)
Mitchell, J.E.
Mitchell, M.S.T.
Brawley, (2)
Kuper, T.P.
Brunson (2)
Young (2)
Rodriguez (2)

Note: (2) indicates both husband and wife.

Sources: Kennedy 1951
Associate Reformed Presbyterian Church 1952-1969

lines of service which begin to emerge once more. The many
short and broken terms surely had adverse results on church
growth. However, in the final analysis, the role which the
missionary fulfills is of more importance than the length of
service.

Meet the Missionaries: The Pioneers

Neill Erskine Pressly: Evangelistic and Medical, 1879-1917.
No matter what one could say about this pioneer in the A. R. P.
work in Mexico it would be insufficient. The difficulties involved in establishing an evangelical mission in Tampico are
treated at length in the first chapter. By 1910, however, the
Tampico congregation had grown to a membership of one hundred
seventeen persons and the church was paying the entire salary
of Rev. Pedro Trujillo. Dr. Pressly, travelling by horseback
into the area south of Tampico, sowed the seed of the Gospel
and at the same time found, taught and commissioned consecrated
men to aid him in preaching in some five stations in outlying
areas. He also founded a school for girls in Tampico. Thinking of the poor who had no medical attention whatsoever at that
time this man of God read medicine for more than a year under
an American doctor of the Railroad Hospital in Tampico. He
then served as physician of body and soul to the poor in the
city and in the area where mission preaching points were begun.
Dr. Pressly was vice-consul of Tampico at the time of the
Revolution, a fact which enabled him to remain except for a
period of a few months in 1914. The following words capture
the spirit of this outstanding missionary:

> Neill E. Pressly was one of the most remarkable men of our
> Church. His faith and courage are apparent in that he set
> foot on a foreign soil and undertook to found a mission,
> backed by a denomination not large in numbers nor rich in
> resources nor trained in experience. Yet he followed his
> convictions, the indications of Providence; he pled for
> his Savior and awakened the sympathy and sustenance of his
> Synod. His devotion to the Mexican Mission is exemplary,
> animating, and sublime (Kennedy 1951:632).

Mrs. Rachel Elliott Pressly: Wife, 1879-1917. Mrs.Pressly
was the helpmate and the counselor of her husband throughout
the thirty-nine years of their pioneer labor in Mexico. In
addition to taking an active part in the work she trained her
children in the fear and admonition of the Lord, educating the
three boys herself. One daughter died in childhood and another
was educated in the United States. One son, Bonner Grier,
became an outstanding minister in the A. R. P. Church; another,
John Ebeneezer was a physician; and the third, Henry Elliott,

served for many years as a missionary of our Church in Mexico.

James Samuel Amzi Hunter: Evangelistic, 1888-1909. Dr. J. S.
A. Hunter spent his time on the mission field in and around
Ciudad del Maiz, S. L. P. (This is the site of the conference
center which is being constructed for the Mexican A. R. P.
Church principally by work-camp groups of young people from the
home church going down during the summer months.) The town was
described by the missionary as a fanatical place and all efforts
to begin a church were met with great opposition. He was stoned
on many occasions. And even as late as 1960 when the first work
camp was held, Catholic opposition to the Protestants was expressed by stones thrown at one of the young people. After two
years of labor a church was organized and by 1903 eighty-two
persons had accepted Christ as Saviour. From the beginning Dr.
Hunter realized the importance of putting the Bible into the
hands of the people. Visiting places in a hundred mile radius
of his station, he organized congregations in San Antonio, Colonia, Minas Viejas and Ciudad Valles.

Mrs. Emma Jane McDill Hunter: Educational, 1888-1901. Mrs.
Hunter was a faithful co-laborer with her husband and her
Christian spirit was felt by many. She was the author of a
small volume of prayers in Spanish. After a short illness Mrs.
Hunter heard the call of her Master and was buried in the city
cemetery of her adopted home.

Martha Ann Grier Boyce: Educational 1891-1896. Miss Mattie
Boyce was appointed by the Board to go to Tampico to help in the
mission effort there. She served as teacher in the Juarez Seminary for Girls. Declining health forced her to return to the
United States against her own wishes.

Mary Parmelia Stevenson: Educational, 1891-1913, 1917-1941.
Miss Macie Stevenson collaborated with Miss Boyce in the Juarez
Seminary for Girls. This school was an important factor in
the acceptance of the evangelicals in Tampico and therefore an
agent of church growth. In addition Miss "Macie" carried on an
active program of home visitation and participated in a most
versatile manner in almost every service of the Mission.

John R. Edwards: Evangelistic, 1893-1907. Dr. Edwards was
the pioneer missionary in Rioverde, S. L. P. On his arrival he
found the same fanaticism, ignorance and folk beliefs which made
the path of the early missionaries difficult in every place where
the seed was being sown. During his ministry there a church
was organized with sixty-four persons on the roll at the end of
fourteen years when Dr. Edwards retired from the field due to
ill health.

Mrs. Amelia Brown Edwards: Educational, 1893-1907. Although
Mrs. Edwards had her hands more than full with her seven children
she gave unstintingly of herself in the mission endeavor. Her
unique service is described like this:

> Seeing the unhappy lot of the numerous orphan children in
> Mexico, for whom no one showed compassion, Mrs. Edwards
> took into her own home a few Mexican children as early as
> 1897, and continued to care for a group of needy ones un-
> til in 1903 friends in the home land were moved to provide
> an ample lot and a suitable building for an orphanage -
> the Hattie Mae Chester Orphanage (Kennedy 1951:616).

When broken health caused the Edwards to leave Mexico, she left
a part of herself in the lives of many with whom she had come
in contact.

Lavinia Neel: Educational, 1894-1913, 1917-1930.

> Clear in vision, steady in purpose, indomitable in her
> manner of serving the Lord and the Church, Miss Lavinia
> Neel gave a lifetime of service in the unspectacular task
> of teaching Mexican girls and boys to be capable citizens
> and good Christians (Kennedy 1951:627).

Miss Neel taught in the mission school at Ciudad del Maiz, the
Hattie Mae Chester Institute in Rioverde and the Juarez Institute in Tampico. Although occupied with school work during her
entire career she found time to do a great deal of visitation
among those who were moving into Tampico. She found a responsive
ness among these migrants to the Gospel.

*James Gary Dale: Evangelistic and Educational, 1899-1913, 1919-
1945.* Dr. Dale felt so strongly the call to foreign service that
he volunteered to go to Mexico trusting the Lord for his financial support. After some months of ministry he was sent to
Rioverde where he established a school to train workers for the
Church. At the time of the Revolution there were sixty men en-
rolled. Following the Revolution Dr. Dale returned to Tampico
where he labored in the planting of churches with a great deal
of success. In 1930, feeling called to minister to the Indians,
he and his wife Dr. Katherine Neel Dale took up that work still
being connected with our Mission until 1945 when he resigned from
the Tampico Presbytery. A discussion of the Indian work can be
found in the first chapter.

Katherine Neel Dale, M. D.: Medical, 1899-1913, 1919-1941.
Katherine Neel Dale was eminently qualified to serve as a
medical missionary, and her years of service in Ciudad del Maiz,

Rioverde, Tampico and Tamanzunchale reaped a rich harvest of
souls for her Lord. This medical work was self-supporting for
the main part and was an important agent in the evangelistic
effort of that day. Going to serve among the Indians with her
husband J. G. Dale, she was supported by the women of the A.R.P.
Church until her death in 1941.

Fannie Lynn Wallace: Educational and Evangelistic, 1900-1902.
Joining the Presslys in Tampico, Miss Wallace soon gained
command of the Spanish language and began to help in the Juarez
Institute for Girls. She also participated in the evangelistic
outreach. Her ministry was cut short by her untimely death on
November 16, 1902.

*Janie Mabel Love: Evangelistic and Educational, 1903-1913,
1922-1945.* Going out to take part in the educational work,
Miss Love served in the schools at Ciudad del Maiz, Rioverde
and Tampico. In 1928 she moved to Ciudad Valles and established an independent mission center beginning with a high
school. Being frustrated in her educational efforts she began
evangelistic work and the story of her success is written in
the number of congregations she formed. Sending out lay workers
and ministers, going herself and being helped by a number of
short-term missionaries, the Gospel took root in twenty-five
villages and towns. Many people in our Church today remember
Miss Love with great esteem. She was a woman of deep faith
and many spiritual qualities, and she contributed greatly to
our work in Mexico.

Mrs. Rosemma Beamer Hunter: Educational, 1903-1913. Mrs.
Hunter was the second wife of Dr. J. S. A. Hunter. She was a
faithful helpmate for him laboring in the school of Rioverde
even after his death, until forced to leave because of the
Revolution. After leaving Mexico she went to Guatemala as a
member of the Central American Mission, working there until her
health failed in 1928.

Martha Anna Strong: Educational, 1903-1906, 1910-1913. Miss
Strong labored in the school in Tampico for three years until
ill health caused her to return to the States. In 1910 she
was able to go back to the field, this time to collaborate with
Mrs. Rosemma Hunter in the educational work in Rioverde. After
leaving Mexico because of the Revolution she never returned.

William Jones Bonner: Educational, 1909-1910. Mr. Bonner
taught for a brief period in the Preparatory School in Rioverde until a severe digestive ailment forced him to return to
the U. S. A.

Mrs. Nelle Rhule Bonner: Wife, 1909-1910. Mrs. Bonner had

little opportunity to participate in the mission endeavor due
to the premature termination of their stay in Mexico.

Jennie Gettys: Educational, 1909-1913. Miss Gettys was sent
to Mexico to take the place of Miss Strong. She labored in the
Juarez Institute in Tampico until the Revolution, after which
she remained in the States.

Henry Elliott Pressly: Evangelistic, 1909-1913, 1923-1939.
Son of our pioneer missionaries, Dr. and Mrs. Neill E. Pressly,
Henry Elliott Pressly took up work among the fanatical people
in Ciudad del Maiz and the surrounding countryside during the
four years prior to the Revolution. After the period of the
Revolution during which time he married, Mr. Pressly returned
and finding Ciudad del Maiz practically destroyed, reopened the
work in Ciudad Valles. The following quote is a striking example of the influence of the Mexican law and of Mr. Pressly's
unique advantage:

> In view of the fact that Mexican law forbids foreign
> ministers to exercise ministerial functions, to facilitate
> his work as a preacher and pastor in Mexico, Mr. Pressly
> in 1927 became a Mexican citizen. It appears that he was
> the only missionary in Mexico who was in a position to
> take this step. Other missionaries preach, but do not
> administer the sacraments (Kennedy 1951:629).

After a number of years of evangelistic work in various parts of
our field the Presslys joined with the Board of the Presbyterian
Church U. S. in their endeavor in Mexico.

Rachel McMaster, M. D.: Medical, 1910-1913. Dr. McMaster was
associated with Dr. Katherine Neel Dale in the medical work in
Rioverde. The Revolution was responsible for her recall to the
United States after which she never returned to Mexico.

W. W. Boyce: Evangelistic, 1912-1913, 1921-1922. When Dr.
Boyce arrived in Mexico the country was already involved in the
pangs of a growing revolution. He went to Tacanhuitz, S. L. P.
where he studied the language and engaged in evangelistic work.
Lack of communication was a major difficulty and when a short-
age of funds forced him to travel to Valles by means of horseback, Dr. Boyce discovered that the other missionaries had already evacuated the country due to the Revolution. He quickly
made arrangements to leave also and did not return until 1921
when the Board asked him to do so. At that time he went back
with his wife and they remained only a short time due to
doctor's orders that Mrs. Boyce be taken back to the States.

Mrs. Lucille Boyce: Wife, 1921-1922. Arriving on the field with her husband in 1921 Mrs. Boyce was advised shortly thereafter to return to the U.S.A. due to illness.

Mrs. Mary Bradley Pressly: Educational, 1923-1939. Mrs. Henry Pressly arrived in Mexico with her husband in 1923. She opened a mission school in Ciudad Valles and was active in the work of the Sabbath School and the women's organization. She and her husband joined with the Presbyterian Church U.S. mission force in Mexico following their furlough in 1939.

Rachel McElroy: Educational, 1925-1935, 1953-1954, 1958-1959. Rachel McElroy volunteered to go to Mexico after two years of experience working in a Daily Bible Kindergarten in Charlotte, North Carolina. She was sent to Rioverde where she was to open a Normal College for the training of Christian teachers. On arrival there she saw some of the results of the Revolution. "The buildings were in unusable condition. They had been used by soldiers who left destruction wherever they went" (McElroy 1969: Letter to author). The Normal College was opened, however, after completing the necessary requirements with the state. Opposition was expressed by some Roman Catholics, but classes were held for nine years until lack of funds and a government requirement that all schools be secularized caused the school to be closed. Miss McElroy returned to the States at that time (1935) having suffered with malaria during most of her stay in Mexico. On two occasions she returned to substitute for missionaries on furlough.

Jesse Miller Dale: Educational, 1926-1927. Jesse Miller Dale worked for only a short time with the A.R.P. Mission in Mexico. He taught in the Juarez School in Tampico where his parents, Dr. and Mrs. J. G. Dale, were residing and working. He returned to the United States because he felt that the laws of Mexico were not favorable to the preaching of the Gospel. At present he is serving in an adjoining field with the Mexican Indian Mission.

John Taylor Dale: Evangelistic, 1932-1935. Dr. John T. Dale joined his parents, Dr. and Mrs. J. G. Dale, in Tamazunchale where they were laboring among the Indians. He never received his salary from the Board of the A.R.P. Church, but for several years did get financial aid on the translation of the Scriptures into the language of the Aztecs. Dr. Dale vanished into the mountains among the Aztecs for an entire year during which time he could not hear a word of English and probably very little Spanish. He translated the Gospel of John into that tongue and is recognized as an authority on his understanding of the Indian. At present he is the associate director of the Mexican Indian Mission.

Mrs. Mabel Poston Dale: Wife, 1943-1945. After the death of
Dr. Katherine Neel Dale, Mabel Poston became the wife of J. G.
Dale joining him in his labors among the Indians.

Meet the Missionaries: The Harvesters

Now we turn to a survey of those missionaries who are at present serving on the field or who have ministered there at some
time during my tenure in Mexico (1961-1970).

*William Chisholm Halliday: Evangelistic and Educational,
1926-*   When William Chisholm Halliday arrived in Mexico in
1926 the country was still recovering from the Revolution. During
his stay there Mexico has become one of the most stable - both
economically and politically - of any of the Latin American
countries. This senior missionary on the field has thus seen
and experienced not only the maturing of a country, but also the
maturing of our mission labors there. In the 1920's there was
some confusion as to the role and function of the ordained
missionary in view of the Mexican law which stated that only
those born in Mexico could officiate as ministers of any religion.
As the responsibilities and privileges were further delineated,
however, Protestant missionaries understood that the native
ministers were expected to perform all the official acts of the
ministry - that is, baptize, administer the Lord's Supper, perform marriages and pronounce the Apostolic benediction, in
addition to being in charge of the congregations. This careful
separation of roles between missionary and national pastor was
acceptable to Dr. Halliday since from the very beginning he had
felt that native leaders must carry the responsibility of
ecclesiastical affairs if a strong Church was to be established.
Most of his missionary career has been spent in the finding and
preparation of national leaders. In 1927 he opened the Rio
Verde Preparatory School for the purpose of preparing ministers
and laymen. Beginning with five pupils in the seventh grade,
there were forty-one students in three grades by 1932. This
school was closed in 1934 when new education laws forbade any
school from receiving support from a religious body. Following
this, Dr. Halliday taught Bible and other subjects to lay preachers who were ministering in the evangelistic district under his
supervision. His active concern during these years was for the
congregations to undertake paying the salaries of their ministers
and for the Tampico Presbytery to take over part of the supervision of the smaller groups. He met with considerable success
in this plan. Later he opened the Rio Verde Bible School which
eventually became the A.R.P. Theological Seminary. (See information on this in Chapter IV.) Dr. Halliday has been responsible
for the training of approximately 90 per cent of our ministers

and lay workers since 1926. His influence is felt throughout
the realm of the A.R.P. Church in Mexico, and his keen insights
make him an invaluable asset to our mission work today.

Mrs. Flora Todd Harper Halliday: Educational, 1926-
Mrs. Halliday as wife, mother, hostess, friend, teacher and
missionary has contributed much to the mission endeavor. In
addition to teaching her three daughters their elementary
schooling, she was on the staff of the Preparatory School and
has given courses in the Seminary. She was one of the founders
of the Federation of Women's Societies of the A.R.P. Church in
Mexico - an organization which has done much to enlist the aid
of the women in the program of the Church. But especially in
the lives of Christian nurses, teachers, secretaries and directors of Christian education do we find the influence of Mrs.
Halliday. She has untiringly supervised and counseled many
young ladies in their quest for a higher education, administering scholarship aid for the Mission. Because of her work in
this sphere an educated leadership is emerging among the Protestant youth. When Dr. and Mrs. Halliday retire in 1971 They
will be missed by missionary and national alike, as their lives
and interests have been intertwined with those of the Mexicans
for many years.

*Robert Alexander Whitesides: Evangelistic and Institutional,
1945-1970.* When Robert Whitesides arrived in Mexico in 1945
the fields were white unto the harvest and the laborers were
few. He and his wife, along with the Hallidays, were the only
missionary personnel. After a period of language study, they
located in Tampico and took up the supervision of the rural
evangelistic work, overseeing ministers and layworkers throughout the surrounding countryside. Mr. Whitesides has continued
with this ministry until the present day. In addition he was
instrumental in the opening of *Las Buenas Nuevas*, a Christian
book store. (See Chapter IV for details of this.) His influence has been deeply felt in the Mexican Synod, where with
diplomacy and wisdom he has played an important role in helping
the Mexican Church grow from infancy to adulthood. His patience
and understanding have brought a cohesiveness to many an explo-
sive situation. After a quarter of a century of work in Mexico,
the Whitesides have rendered their resignation, effective June
30, 1970, feeling that the time when they can contribute to the
growth of the Church has now come to an end. They will be sorely
missed as we labor in the immediate future towards the goal of
an autonomous Church.

Mrs. Harriett Lou Robinson Whitesides: Business, 1945-1970.
As the mother of six children, Robert, Daniel, Harriett, Daisy,

Rebecca and James, Mrs. Whitesides has had a fulltime job. Her family is a credit to the Christian training they have received at home. In addition Harriett has served as mission treasurer for a number of years and has joined with the Mexicans in the work of the local church and in work among the women. The following expresses her thoughts concerning the increasing role of the national workers.

> I firmly believe that people only grow and mature to the extent that the responsibility is placed upon them. The Mexicans must in time assume the entire responsibility for their church here if it is to stand (Whitesides, H. L. 1969: Letter to author).

Patrick G. Covone: Evangelistic and Educational, 1951- .
Coming from an Italian Roman Catholic family in New Jersey, Pat Covone was converted to the Protestant faith while attending Erskine College, Due West, South Carolina. He had planned to be a Catholic priest, but instead God called him into the Protestant ministry. In 1951 he and his wife were sent to Mexico, the first missionaries to go to the field in six years. His Italian ancestry and upbringing have prepared him in a unique way to serve among the Latin Americans, reducing the cultural gap and thus increasing his ability to communicate. Pat oversees the Sara Flores Home for Boys, a hostel for elementary pupils. We hope that these students will be our church leaders tomorrow, especially in the rural areas from where they come. Pat also supervises our ministry among the Aztec and Huastec Indians. Although he does not speak these languages himself - anymore than do our ordained Mexican ministers - he selects lay workers who can speak the "heart" language of the Indians to labor among them. In addition he supervises several preaching points among the Spanish-speaking people. He has encouraged the congregations in all these smaller preaching points to build their own churches. Pat has promised to provide the roof if the people lay the foundations and put up the walls. In most of these areas he has been able to place some type of portable organ to provide instrumental music in the services, something that the Mexicans love. Pat's success may be in great part attributed to the fact that his identification with the Mexicans is so complete that he feels more "at home" with these brothers in Christ than in the United States.

Mrs. Imogene Edmunds Covone: Evangelistic and Educational, 1951- . Although the mother of three children (Phillip, Gina and Cathy) whom she teaches at home part of the time, Imogene contributes much to the mission cause. She supervises the Janie Love Home, a hostel for primary age girls. She has been a source of inspiration and guidance in the local church, participating in the jail ministry and in the organization of a new congregation in a suburb of the city. On the Synodical level, she has had a direct role in the organization of several local women's societies and is looked to for spiritual leadership. Her magnificent control of the Spanish language is a definite asset in her missionary labors.

James Erskine Mitchell: Business and Evangelistic, 1961-. Feeling that God was calling him to the mission field during his involvement in a work camp in Mexico in July, 1960, the author made his application to the Board and was sent to the field following his graduation from Erskine College in 1961. He has served as administrator of the Neill E. Pressly Clinic and has been engaged in the local church work and the evangelistic effort of the Mission throughout the Synod.

Mrs. Martha Sue Taylor Mitchell: Christian Education, 1963- Collaborating with her husband in the medical mission effort as well as in the evangelistic thrust on the local and rural areas, Martha Sue has contributed in a number of ways to the mission enterprise. They have two children, Deborah Sue and James Erskine, Jr.

Robert Lawson Brawley: Educational and Evangelistic, 1965-1968. Going as a short-term missionary, Robert did an admirable job in learning the Spanish language in the little time that was given him for study. He worked with the Seminary in Rioverde in addition to supervising preaching points in the states of San Luis Potosi and Tamaulipas. A faithful preacher of the Word, he was able to communicate God's message to the Mexican people in a meaningful way.

Mrs. Jane Amelia Patrick Brawley: Wife, 1965-1968. The mother of two girls, Anna and Sara, Jane provided the influence and the example of a Christian home.

Mrs. Theodosia Profitt Kuper: Housemother, 1965, 1968- As an answer to prayer, Mrs. Kuper went to Mexico to serve as housemother for the nurses working in the Neill E. Pressly Clinic. Both her willingness to leave her homeland and her vibrant Christian personality have been an inspiration to all with whom she comes in contact. Her being present as housemother has provided the ingredient which makes a house a Christian home. Her role is that of witness by work and by counsel.

Ronnie Leon Brunson: Business and Evangelistic, 1968- Ronnie's arrival in Mexico as a missionary was the fulfillment of a dream. He is serving at present as administrator of the

Neill E. Pressly Clinic. After the author's return to the field, Mr. Brunson hopes to concentrate on the evangelistic effort.

Mrs. Pamela Mohlman Brunson: Medical, 1968-   Pam, a registered nurse, is eminently prepared to share with her husband in the missionary endeavor. They are the parents of two children, Andrew and Beth Ellen.

Lawrence C. Young: Evangelistic, 1968-1969. Going to Mexico to take up an evangelistic ministry in the state of Vera Cruz, Larry located in the city of Tuxpam after completing his language study. Due to the almost continual illness of his family, he was recalled after a short time.

Mrs. Sue Young: Wife, 1968-1969. Sue and their three children, Robin, Amy and Lawrence, Jr., were unable to take an active part in the mission enterprise because of illness which forced their return to the States.

David Rodriguez Enriquez, M. D.: Medical 1969-   David Rodriguez is the son of a retired lay worker. From youth his desire was to have a share in the mission effort in a medical sense. Receiving his schooling on a mission scholarship, he has been associated with the Neill E. Pressly Clinic since its beginning in 1959. His practice required much time away from the clinic, however, and in 1969 he made application to the Board to serve as a missionary to his own people. His acceptance made him the first national missionary in the history of the A.R.P. Church in Mexico.

Mrs. Lucia A. de Rodriguez: Wife, 1969-   . Lucia, an active participant in the program of the local church in every phase, brings a new perspective to the mission force as she supports her husband in the medical aspect and as she ministers among her own people. The Rodriguez family has three sons, David, Daniel and Andres.

Learn of Their Task

In retrospect it is noted that the Associate Reformed Presbyterian Church has sent forty-two missionaries to Mexico from the United States in a period of ninety years. Two missionaries from Mexico have been commissioned by the Board to serve their own people, making a total of forty-four. These forty-four have been located in the states of Tamaulipas and San Luis Potosi, with the exception of one couple who were in Vera Cruz for less than one year. Their spheres of activity have been chiefly institutional though almost all have shared in the evangelistic effort to some degree or other. Some have concentrated on planting churches, some in training leaders for these churches and others in serving the Christian community and the Mexican people in general.

What then is a missionary? Some people think of him as superhuman or a little "god." He should and indeed must be one who is deeply consecrated to his Lord, but at the same time he is just as human and has the same human feelings, needs and desires as anyone else. The missionary is a Christian human being. The word Christian means "Christ-like" or one who follows Christ. He loves God and therefore loves his fellow man. Here again the missionary is no different from other Christians.

Probably the only difference between rank and file Christians and the ordinary missionary is that the missionary has received a call from God to witness and serve among another people and has had the grace to accept such a calling. God calls each one of us to a task and gives us the power to fulfill it. No one can boast because it is a gift from God. The missionary, like the apostle of old and the Christian of any age, should be one who is completely dedicated to the Lord Jesus Christ, a man of faith, one who believes the Word of God and one who expects results when ministering in the name of Jesus.

What is the role of the missionary? Our early missionaries were ministers, and functioned as such in Mexico. They laid the foundation and drew the designs for the development of the A.R.P. Church. Their control and influence were quite evident in those early stages. Soon they felt the need to participate in educational work, and in those formative years the Protestant schools were instruments of good will and helped obtain entrance into many closed doors. Medical work was also an important part of the mission endeavor; the early missionaries felt that it was the single most important factor in the growth of the Church in those first struggling years.

With the adoption of the Constitution of 1917 our missionaries could no longer serve officially as ministers. However, the Church was not adversely affected since this new Constitution only legally enforced what was already common practice: as soon as nationals were trained they were placed in charge of congregations. The new education laws forced our Mission to abandon the operation of secondary and elementary schools; this was probably a blessing in disguise for it caused the missionaries to dedicate their time to the training of lay workers and ministers.

Until 1945, however, the role of the missionary was still

that of the leader, the one in control, and the national was in
the background. In that year the "Plan of Cooperation" was
put into effect, and the national began to emerge with greater
responsibility, taking upon his shoulder a larger part of the
ministry and feeling that this was his Church. The missionary
still had power and influence through his membership in the Presbytery, but he was no longer the all-important force in the Church.

As the Church continued to grow and a separate Mexican Synod
was formed in 1964, the reins of leadership passed into the
hands of the nationals and the missionary began to fade into the
background. Robert Whitesides stated in a mission meeting that
even as John the Baptist said that he must decrease and Christ
increase, we as missionaries should decrease while the role of
the nationals increases. This then is the period in which we
are at the present time, and the role of the missionary is
changing from that of partner to that of servant. See Plate 18
showing the typology of missionary roles.

It is to be clarified, however, that this chart only refers
to the emergence of a national Church. No reference is made to
the need of an emerging Mexican mission operation that would be
related to the Mexican national Church just as is our U. S.
Church Extension Department related to our U. S. A.R.P. Church.
No doubt the emergence of a sister Church in Mexico must elicit
direct formal diplomatic ties between the leadership of the
two churches, rather than a relation between the leaders of the
Mexican Church and the leaders of the U. S. A.R.P. Mission.
Clearly then the emergence of a national Church does not mean
the end of mission outreach in Mexico. Properly conceived, our
U. S. A.R.P. Mission and a yet-to-be-developed Mexican mission
department have great challenges before them in joint (and perhaps even separate) church planting in the years to come. In
regard to the running of the new Mexican Church, however, the
Mexican alone must carry the chief responsibilities. There is
widespread misunderstanding on this question, since many con-
fuse the nature of properly diminishing the mission-to-church
relations with the essentially different and continuing re-
lationships of mission-to-mission and church-to-church. Otherwise initiative in the expansion of the faith may be tragically
lost.

The missionary is still needed on our mission field in the
Latin American situation. All the fields have not been harvested. There are still many places where churches should be
planted. As never before the missionary needs an increased
understanding of his role as a church multiplier as well as a
knowledge of how to accomplish this in the decade of the 70's.
He is also needed in certain areas of administration and in

PLATE 18

TYPOLOGY OF MISSIONARY ROLES

Mission Relationship to Church	Stage of Church Development				
	PIONEER	EMERGING CHURCH	COOPERATION	BEGINNING AUTONOMY	FINAL AUTONOMY
OUTSIDER	APOSTOLATE				
OUTSIDE CONTROL		ADMINISTRATOR			
INTEGRAL PART OF NATIONAL CHURCH			PARTNER		
INVITED MINISTRY				SERVANT	
AGENT OF INTER-CHURCH MINISTRY					CONSULTANT

Source: Read, Monterroso and Johnson 1969:292

(Used by permission of Wm. B. Eerdmans Publishing Co. from *Latin American Church Growth*.)

positions where specialized skills are required. However, the
missionary must never forget that he is expendable and that his
role today demands flexibility. As he seeks for success in
his missionary efforts, the words of Eugene Nida are meaningful:

> However, a close examination of successful missionary
> work inevitably reveals the correspondingly effective
> manner in which the missionaries were able to identify
> themselves with the people 'to be all things to all men'-
> and to communicate their message in terms which have
> meaning for the lives of the people (Nida 1954:250).

The A.R.P. missionary in Mexico is faced with a challenge to
move forward in the extension of the Church with the leadership of his brothers in Christ.

THE ROLE OF THE NATIONAL

The Minister

Matthew 9:37 (R. S. V.) says: "Then he said to his disciples,
'The harvest is plentiful, but the laborers are few.'" Never
in the history of the Associate Reformed Presbyterian Church in
Mexico has there been a sufficient number of ministers. In
the early years if a convert seemed interested and capable of
becoming a minister, the missionary would give him the necessary
training. In most cases the instruction was imparted in the
aspirant's own village or by correspondance, and usually for a
very short time. The young man would then be licensed to
preach and in some cases later ordained. Some of these ministers had very little formal education; others had completed
various levels of schooling. The training and preparation of
two of the pioneer ministers were described in the following
manner:

> Guadalupe Cruz never attended school. His father taught
> him to read and with an ambition to learn, he used the
> few books that fell into his hands and acquired a useful
> stock of information ... He read the Bible from Genesis
> to Revelation.
> Cresenciano Cruz was sent to the States for his educa-
> tion. His literary course was pursued at Erskine College
> and he was graduated from the Theological Seminary in
> 1898 (Dale 1910:129-130).

In 1910 nine national ministers were in the service of our
Church. In 1970 we have only twelve. There are several

reasons for this lack of ministers: 1) Educational requirements.
To enter the seminary for ministerial training an aspirant must
have completed preparatory school having an equivalent of two
years of college. This seriously reduces the number of those
who are eligible. 2) Salary Schedule. Men in other jobs with
a similar amount of schooling earn from two thousand ($160 U.S.)
to ten thousand ($800 U.S.) pesos per month. With one or two
exceptions our ministers earn little more than half of the
minimum the others get, or only one thousand one hundred pesos
per month ($88 U.S.). 3) Small Number of Communicants. The
A.R.P. Church in Mexico has only 2,389 communicants, and as a
consequence very few become ministers.

The ministers who are serving as pastors of congregations
are deeply dedicated men and well trained. It is recognized
that as the leaders on the local level they are key figures in
the growth of the Church. Their role is a varied one. Under
the Mexican law, and wisely so, they must carry the responsibility of the official duties of the ministry. The majority
of our ordained men are in charge of large city churches. Several of these churches have planted other congregations, either
within the city or in the surrounding rural community, and
temporarily at least the minister must pastor these charges as
well. In addition the ministers have responsibilities with
the Presbytery and the Synod. Many have to visit six or more
preaching points to oversee the ministry there and they are
called upon to travel a distance of eighty miles or more to
baptize, officiate at the Lord's Supper or perform a marriage
ceremony. Some teach in our seminary in Rioverde. Amador
Pesina G. has travelled three hundred miles each month to give
one course, and Maurilio Lopez has travelled as much as four
hundred miles.

All of the ministers are overworked, burning the candle at
both ends. Yet at the same time they are intensely committed
to the Gospel and to the propagation of the good news to every
person. On such strength the Church finds much potential for
growth. Matthew 9:37 (R. S. V.) clearly expresses our concern:
"Pray therefore the Lord of the harvest to send out laborers
into his harvest."

The Paid Lay Worker

In speaking of patterns of ministry not commonly found in the
United States, perhaps some definitions would be in order. A
preaching point (or a mission station as it is often called in
A.R.P. circles) is a congregation which has not yet reached the
status of being an organized church. A village, ranch or small

town is visited. A group or family of Christians may be found
without ecclesiastical structure. Or there may be only one
individual who is interested in the Gospel and willing for services to be held in his home. Thus a mission is begun with no
members or with very few. It is hoped that over the years
these congregations will increase numerically and in their ability to be self-supporting so that a church might be organized.

The lay worker is the Christian man or woman sent out to
minister in these areas. Many lay workers have little schooling,
but are dedicated Christians, called into the service of God.
Without their efforts the work of the Church would suffer. The
pay scale for the lay worker is six hundred pesos per month
($48 U.S.).

A large number of paid lay workers are serving in the Associate
Reformed Presbyterian Church in Mexico under the supervision of
the *Junta Unida de Misiones Domesticas*, a joint home missions
board made up of national ministers and three missionaries. This
joint committee has control of all the preaching points and the
lay workers who man them, although some of the workers are still
paid by the missionary and, in a sense, work for him. Until recently the congregations which were able to contribute a certain
percentage of the lay worker's salary were under the direct
supervision of one of the three presbyteries and the others were
under the supervision of the Mission. This situation created
loyalties to personalities and fostered the idea that the lay
worker was working for the "north American" rather than for the
church. This feeling was reduced with the formation of the
joint committee, which consists of both missionaries and nationals and which has the task of placing lay workers, setting up
their pay schedules, and in general providing a unanimity of
role among them.

Each year one or two training institutes are held for the lay
workers. On occasions seminary courses are offered to them in
schools lasting from one to three months.

The paid lay worker has been an important person in the
ministry of the Church in Mexico. He evangelizes, preaches,
teaches and will probably continue to be a key figure in the
planting of churches for some time to come.

The Layman

The laity as known in the United States has not had a great
role in the founding and operation of our Church in Mexico,
and this may possibly be one of the biggest mistakes that has

been made. As was true in our Church in the States in early
years, it was the custom in Mexico for the minister, the missionary and the paid lay worker to do everything. The trend has begun to shift, and in Mexico the laymen are now realizing that
the Church cannot grow as it should unless "all the faithful"
join in the army of Christ.

This importance of the participation of the laity in the life
and work of the Church cannot be overemphasized. It is vital
to have elders, deacons, teachers, youth workers, choir singers,
committee members, treasurers, and so the list could go on.
Above all, it is essential to the growth of the Church to have
a laity which is actively involved in the task of evangelism.
One of the reasons behind the fast growth of the Pentecostal
groups in Latin America at the present time is the fact that
the evangelistic effort is considered to be the responsibility
and privilege of every believer.

In a static church, the goal is the status quo. No one -
minister or layman - tries to proclaim an evangel which converts.
In a slow growing situation, there may be one or two people who
are witnessing and winning some few to Christ and bringing them
into the fold of God's people. Where churches have spread
rapidly across the country in New Testament fashion, laymen have
often been found to be the agents of that extension. Figures
speak for themselves as to the phenomenal effect this can have
on church growth. Take for example a congregation with one
hundred members where four laymen are enthusiastic workers. If
each brings into the fellowship an average of one new member
per month the church achieves a 48 per cent rate of growth in
one year. The averages soar as more and more of the laymen
participate and produce results.   We need then a great body
of Christian youth and adults who know why they are Christian
and who are trained to proclaim the good news of salvation to
the unsaved around them and convince them that the Christian
faith should be accepted. Such activity on the part of the
laymen will produce church growth.

The laymen of the A.R.P. Church in Mexico are becoming more
active. In Tampico the young peoples' groups were well received
when they evangelized a new *colonia*, a suburb of the city. They
soon outgrew the house in which they were holding weekly services and the *Esfuerzo Cristiano* requested a loan from the
Mission in order to construct a suitable building. The request
was granted, and at last report the young people and the growing church were faithfully repaying the money. This is a striking example of the contribution of the youth to church growth.

The women through their organization, the *Sociedad Femenil*,

are taking part in the outreach of the Church. In some places
the women have begun Bible study groups within the local jails;
others have been concerned with helping another group start
a woman's society; and some have planted congregations even
taking the responsibility for visitation and teaching.

The men, as concerned individuals, are now taking more of a
share in the work of the Church. On their days off work, some
visit one of the small missions and preach. They receive no
remuneration for this. Others who are professional men, such
as doctors, give of their time and talents to help people in
villages where there is no medical attention. In addition to
treating the sick they often preach.

One of our missionaries has expressed the idea that the future growth of our Church is going to depend more and more on
the participation of the laity in the work of the Church. It
is a valid conclusion.

The Relation Between National and Missionary

Having considered the role of the missionary and the national
we now face the question of how they work together.

> The crucial level of interaction between Church and mission
> is the working relationship of missionaries and nationals,
> since it is at this level that theory becomes practice.
> The personal relationships involved affect church growth
> far more directly than the theoretical relationship of
> the mission to the Church (Read, Monterroso and Johnson
> 1969:294).

In a penetrating novel, Juan M. Isais has pulled back the
curtain on the relationship between missionary and national.
Though perhaps not speaking of any one Mission or Church in
particular, his analysis of the problems as expressed in *The
Other Side of the Coin* is revealing of situations common to
missions and national churches around the world.

The national sees the missionary as one who fails to identify with the country and the people. He spends more time in
seeming trivialities than with the work for which he was sent.
"Go ye into all the world, take pictures, and write letters to
every creature" (Isais 1966:44). The missionary seems to
assume a condescending attitude toward the national. Remembering past mistakes, he gives authority and then usurps it,
often asking of the national what he is not prepared to do
himself.

On the other hand, the missionary pictures the national as one who is careless about punctuality, about the fulfillment of obligations and about his appearance. He appears to take no interest in furthering his education. He borrows money and "forgets" to repay it. He seems insincere in his relationship with the missionary.

Certainly no one missionary nor national fits this picture completely, but when these traits exist and are misunderstood, or impatiently handled, barriers are created. It must be agreed that missionary-national cooperation is a necessity, and as it comes about the possibilities for church growth increase and broaden.

THE ROLE OF THE INTERDENOMINATIONAL SOCIETIES

There are many interdenominational "service" missions which assist in various specialized ways in the work of the Kingdom of God in Mexico. Their role is not that of establishing churches, but rather that of providing aid to those missions, national churches and individuals who are engaged in this labor. Some of these organizations are familiar to everyone, but many are unknown either to ministers, laymen or missionaries. See list of addresses in Appendix B. Not all of the interdenominational societies working in Mexico are included in this discussion. Some are omitted because, although their support base is interdenominational in the United States, their work is like that of our own Church to form a denomination in Mexico.

La Sociedad Bíblica de México. The Mexican Bible Society was begun by the efforts of the American Bible Society. Until recently it was still a part of this mother organization.

La Sociedad Bíblica serves and is backed by all of the Protestant groups in Mexico. Its ministry is similar to that being carried on in the States. It supervises translations and revisions of the Scriptures, but its primary endeavor is to print and distribute the Bible and other Christian literature at a nominal price. The entire Bible can be bought in Spanish for ten pesos (.80 U.S.). Portions of the Bible can be bought for as little as two cents. The ministry of the Sociedad Bíblica fills a very important place in the work of the Church in Mexico. The Word of God is essential for an evangelistic movement in both the small mission and in the large organized church and it is equally important for the Christian nuture of the believer.

The Evangelical Foreign Missions Association. This

organization, a division of the National Association of Evangelical Churches in the U.S.A., is not a mission in the usual sense
but is an association of mission agencies, and is open for membership to the missions of the denominational Churches and interdenominational missions. It has sixty-five member missions (ten
associate members) with 7,111 missionaries and 33,000 nationals
represented. The main objectives are:

1. United representation before the government.
2. A basis for fellowship.
3. Cooperative effort.
4. Information governing regulation and international
   affairs which affect missionaries.
5. Service for securing passports, legal documents, travel
   reservations, equipment, supplies, and an information
   service (Missionary Research Library 1968:VII-3).

*The Interdenominational Foreign Mission Association of North
America, Inc.* The IFMA was founded before the Evangelical
Foreign Missions Association and unlike the latter does not have
any denominational societies in its membership, but has a similar
size and function. Its member mission agencies "are engaged in
the vital task of bringing the Gospel of the Lord Jesus Christ
to all people everywhere (Missionary Research Library 1968:VII-
4). The IFMA was formed in 1917 to assist the so called "faith
missions." It grew out of a need for the mission leaders to
meet together from time to time for prayer, consultation and
mutual exchange of ideas pertaining to mission work.

As time progressed so did the IFMA. It discovered that there
were other advantages in being such an association. The IFMA
could give guidance on matters of missionary strategy, on presenting the cause of missions on the home front, on producing
better candidates for service and on reducing the number of
missionary casualties. Its fields lie in three areas: 1) a
mission information service; 2) providing independent missionary
leadership; 3) promotion of evangelistic cooperation. A summary
statement says:

> In recent years, because of its sound and spiritual leader-
> ship, its sane principles and policies of missionary work,
> its solid achievements on the mission field, its continued
> emphasis on evangelism and the indigenous church as well
> as its strong evangelical position, the IFMA has, through
> no choice of its own, taken on the aspect of an accrediting
> association in the field of interdenominational missions
> (Kane 1956:11).

The Gideons International. The Gideons International had its

beginning in 1895 when two Christian businessmen were placed in
the same hotel room. After having devotions together they
talked about the possibility of forming an organization for men
such as themselves. The idea materialized to be one of great
importance all over the world. The objectives of the Gideons
are stated as follows:

1. To associate Christian businessmen for service.
2. To win men and women for the Lord Jesus Christ.
3. To place the Bible - God's Holy Word - in hotels, hos-
   pitals, schools, institutions and other places (Westburg 1959:51).

The Gideons strongly encourage personal evangelism along
with the distribution of the Scriptures. Members of the A.R.P.
Church in Mexico have testified of their witness and of their
effective labor in that country.

Gospel Films, Inc. Gospel Films, Inc. supplies films in
twenty-five languages to missionaries in one hundred twelve
countries and territories. Since the films are sent free of
charge, an effort is made to make them available to missionaries
in every area of the world. They are evangelistically oriented
and quite effective to gather a crowd. The possibility of
using these films in the evangelistic campaigns in our Church
in Mexico, particularly in the rural areas, bears investigation.

Gospel Recordings, Inc. Gospel Recordings, Inc. was begun
by Joy Ridderhof, a missionary to Honduras from Los Angeles,
California. At the end of her first six years on the field,
Joy's health was already failing. While in Los Angeles re-
cuperating, she began to think of her mission field and the many
people who had heard no more than a mention of the Gospel, or
perhaps nothing at all. Joy remembered the sounds of gramophone records that were played in saloons and other stores of
Honduras. Why not use a gramophone record to preach the Gospel? Songs could be recorded too. She remembered the times
when she had been tired on the mission field, and thought of
the records which could be used in thousands of places at the
same time without growing tired. She became convinced that
records could be an avenue to make the Gospel available to
many more people.

On December 31, 1938, the first record was produced. Joy
grew very excited about the project, and although in poor health
and in meager financial straits, she acted in faith. She was
confident that the Lord who had provided in the past would send
the means for this project. Arrangements were made for those
who had spoken Spanish from youth to make the recordings so

that they would sound like national productions.

With this small beginning the Gospel Recordings society was organized. It has grown and now serves in many areas throughout the world. The facility of using the recordings and the excellency of the productions call for their inclusion in our field of service.

Heifer Project, Inc. This association works mainly with the rural people giving them cattle, goats, hogs, chickens and rabbits, whether Protestant or not. Heifer Project, under an agreement with the Mexican government, imports the highest quality of animals into the country for distribution. Several persons in our church fellowship have benefitted from this service. Recently problems have arisen concerning the importation papers, and the association is considering moving to another Latin American country.

Laubach Literacy Fund, Inc. The Laubach method originated with Dr. Frank Laubach and is known throughout the world as "each one teach one." The idea actually sprang from the words of one of the Moros in Lanao who told Dr. Laubach that everyone who was taught to read would have to teach another or he would kill them. The method was put into practice and it spread like wildfire.

This system has been used extensively in Mexico since 1943. The percentage of illiteracy was quite high in the country at that time. Thus the Laubach principle was valuable for both the country and the Church. In the three states where the A.R.P. Church is working, statistics show that in 1960 there were 2,282,500 people who could read and 1,568,500 who could not read (Zertuche 1963:33). The importance for the Christian of being able to read the Bible cannot be overlooked. The Laubach method should be used to the fullest both for those within and without the Christian community.

The Mexican Militant Mission, Inc. The Mexican Militant Mission, Inc. is an international independent faith mission supported by free will offerings of God's people. Since its incorporation in 1954 it has proclaimed the Gospel in various ways. One of its recent important ministries is that of Bible correspondence courses. Another is the broadcasting of Gospel programs over radio throughout the Mexican Republic. Weekly programs are transmitted in Monclova, Coahuila; Puebla, Puebla; Sabinas, Coahuila; and Nuevo Laredo, Tamaulipas. Although interdenominational in its organization, a national denomination known as the Evangelical Missionary Church has emerged from the Mexican Militant Mission in Mexico.

The Navigators. The Navigators is an interdenominational Christian organization which concentrates on winning and training men and women for Christian service. It was begun in Southern California in 1933, and its first overseas work was started in Shanghai in 1949. Today the Navigators serve in twenty-four countries around the world. Those sent out by the Navigators usually work in training centers where many people, mainly youth, receive help in their daily application of scriptural principles. They emphasize the memorization of God's Word and have several courses available for people of all ages and in all stages of Christian growth.

Overseas Crusades, Inc. The Overseas Crusade team in Mexico uses radio and television as its main vehicle to preach the Gospel. There are many advantages to a radio ministry. Because a radio can be found in almost every home in Mexico, more people may be reached with the message in one day than a single Christian can speak to in a lifetime.

The first television campaigns of the Overseas Crusades held in Mexico were in Tampico, Tamaulipas and Villahermosa, Tabasco. It hopes soon to establish a continental television crusade on the Billy Graham style. Some of the members of our denomination have testified that they were first reached by the Gospel through radio or television.

Scripture Gift Mission. The Scripture Gift Mission sends portions of the Scripture and tracts free of charge to those who request them. The only condition is that if the literature is sold, the proceeds should be sent to them. All material is very attractively presented and has been used by the author on numerous occasions in evangelistic campaigns and in the clinic ministry.

World Literature Crusade. This organization is known for its systematic "every-home" crusade. Its objective is to get the printed Gospel message into each home of the world. It plants the seed which others may reap.

Wycliffe Bible Translators, Inc. As implied in its name, the Wycliffe Bible translators has dedicated itself to translating the Bible into the language of the common people. Between 100 A.D. and 1450 A.D. the Scripture appeared in thirty-three languages, one new language every forty years. By 1750 there were translations in seventy-one more tongues, an average of one every nine years. Between 1801 and 1830 with the help of William Carey and others, translations in eighty-six more languages were produced, three per year. From 1831 to 1837 851 more languages received the Bible for the first time, or

eight per year. At the present time there is an average of
one new translation coming off the press every three weeks.

In Mexico there are eighty-eight languages other than Spanish, not all of which have a translation of the Bible. The
job of making the Scripture available to such different groups
requires much labor. The steps followed by the translators are
these:

1. Learning the spoken language.
2. Reducing the language to writing and making scientifi-
   cally correct alphabets, dictionaries and grammars.
3. Long years of tedious translating.
4. The costly business of preparing and testing, pre-publi-
   cation, impressing of the manuscript. (Publication is
   in most cases undertaken by the American Bible Society
   which works in close cooperation with the Wycliffe
   Bible Translators.)
5. Conducting reading campaigns, preparing primers, charts,
   and other reading aids (Kane 1956:164).

There are several other interdenominational societies working in Mexico which provide similar services to the ones discussed in this chapter. Information about them may be obtained
by writing to the addresses listed in Appendix B.

The role then of all these societies is that of providing
background support in the on-going task of winning Mexico for
Christ. The missions which have the task of establishing a
national Church which will continue to grow and multiply
should be aware of and make use of the many opportunities for
assistance which the interdenominational societies offer.

6

Future Outlook

TRENDS SINCE VATICAN II

When Pope John XXIII announced on January 25, 1959, that he would call a general council of the Roman Catholic Church, the eyes of the world began to turn toward Rome. What would this historical event mean, not only for Roman Catholics, but for all Christians?

Vatican II covered a period of three years - from October, 1962 to December, 1965. It was begun by Pope John XXIII, already in his eighties, and was completed by Pope Paul VI. It has provoked much discussion throughout Christendom. Its accomplishments and significance cannot be understood only in the context of the history of the Roman Catholic Church, because events emanating from Vatican II have confronted all churches with new problems and decisions. The Church in Mexico is no exception.

Effects on the Roman Catholic Church

One of the fundamental themes of Vatican II was expressed in the word *aggiornamento,* which signifies updating, or "an evangelical attitude toward the present with all the concrete possibilities of salvation that it affords" (Haring 1966:13). Vatican II was marked by the desire for reform and renewal. It resulted in a changed climate in the Roman Catholic Church even though many of the dogmas remained the same and some of the desired achievements were not accomplished. Several of the reforms proposed were immediately noticed in the Church in

Mexico, affecting the life and work of the Catholics there.

Back to the Bible. For many years priests discouraged the
average Roman Catholic laymen in Mexico from reading the Bible.
The people were told that the Scriptures were only for the
clergy. The priests were to read, study and expound the meaning of God's Word, and it was unnecessary for the laymen to
do so. It was unthinkable for the common people to be able to
understand the Book.

After Vatican II, the atmosphere changed considerably. The
Church now distributes the Catholic version of the Bible and
even allows the reading of Protestant translations. An effort
has been made to put the Scriptures into the hands of the
people. Noticeable in the stores of Mexico are the counters
with Bibles for sale. In Tampico in a popular variety store,
there was a counter filled with paper back copies of the American Bible Society's *Dios Llega al Hombre,* which is similar to
Good News for Modern Man, located right at the cash register
where everyone would see it. Some of the Catholics have been
asking the question: "Why have the Protestants had God's Word
to read for over one hundred years in Mexico and we are just
now receiving it?" It is a question which cannot be answered
to the satisfaction of the thinking person.

With the new emphasis on the Bible, the priests are making
more of an effort to present messages based on Scripture rather
than doctrinal sermons. Bible study groups have grown up in
some areas. Out of these have come still more questions and
an amazement about Protestant friends who are so well versed
in matters of the Bible.

The Mass in Spanish. For over four centuries the Mexican
people had listened to the mass in Latin. Meaning little to
the speaker and less to the hearer, the service was a matter of
ritual. There is no doubt that some were moved by the pomp
and ceremony, but the majority understood little if any of what
was taking place. Then Vatican II gave permission for the mass
to be spoken in the vernacular of the people, a truly revolutionary aspect of the Catholic renewal.

Brotherhood. Before Vatican II the Protestants were regarded
as "schismatics." Even with freedom of religion and protection
by the neutral Mexican government, the evangelical minority
could not always be assured of nonviolence. At least one of the
missionaries presently on the field has been stoned on one
occasion. In 1948 in the little village of San Diego, S.L.P.,
an ex-Catholic priest was speaking in the A.R.P. Church when a
mob of at least one hundred twenty men and women came down the

hill from the Roman Catholic Church, forced their way into the
A.R.P. chapel and attempted to break up the meeting. The little
ten year old son of the former lay preacher in that village lost
his life shortly thereafter in a violent manner. His body was
found in an orange grove.

> Rope burns marked the body and arms; one arm was out of
> joint, and the head was turned 180 degrees, looking back-
> ward. Furthermore the body showed 80 tiny perforations,
> such as might be made by an ice pick or very large needle
> (Halliday 1969-1970: Private correspondence).

Other antagonism has been felt, less violently but just as
active.

Down With the Idols. Some Roman Catholic churches in Mexico
are progressively removing the images from their sanctuaries.
The much celebrated act of the priest in Cuernavaca, Morelos
who threw out all the images in his church in 1963 is a case in
point. Others have followed his example. However, many of the
images are still left untouched.

The Protestant who arrives in Mexico at the time of one of
the religious festivals cannot help but be amazed at the imagery
in these activities. The virgin Mary, as mentioned earlier, is
the object of the greatest veneration. Even today the entire
month of May is focused on the Virgin. Small girls are dressed
in the traditional color of virginity, white, and are taken to
the cathedral to offer flowers to the "mother of God."

Other Significant Effects. Several other documents which
came out of Vatican II bear mentioning. One of these dealt with
the Church, bringing forth a new concept of its being the Body
of Christ. The Holy Spirit was seen as the real protagonist,
activating and cementing that which was decided by the Council.

Surely much was said and done during those three history
making years. Results will continue to be felt by various
branches of the Roman Catholic Church in different parts of the
world as the decisions are assimilated by the clergy and the
laity and are put into action.

Effects on the Protestant Church

How did the Second Vatican Council affect the life and work
of the evangelicals in Mexico? To answer this we must first
ascertain what has been the relationship between the Catholics
and the evangelical Churches. The Roman Catholic faith, as

introduced by the Spanish conquerors, has been the predominant faith of the people. To be Mexican has been almost synonymous with being Roman Catholic. The Protestant minority, although guaranteed religious freedom by the government, has suffered persecution from the dominant Church.

It is clear that the Roman Church considered the Protestant penetration of Mexico an unnecessary and unwanted intrusion. The Protestants on the other hand felt the Catholic faith to be less than adequate:

> Some Catholics are Christians in spite of their church. But to the rest the personal Christ is hidden behind an impenetrable curtain of privilege and pomp, sacerdotalism and sacraments (Wagner 1969:21).

The first and foremost effect of Vatican II on the Protestant movement in Mexico has been the change in attitude and atmosphere. By the acceptance of members of non-Catholic churches as separated brethren, the stigma of being an evangelical has been at least partially removed. Without question this has made it easier for some to enter the Protestant Church. It must not be assumed, however, that the face of the Roman Catholic Church in Mexico has so greatly changed that there has been a dramatic move toward Protestantism. There are still areas where Catholic churches retain the position of supremacy, and totally ignore other churches, and the attitude of Vatican II has not automatically become the attitude of all the Mexican people. Nevertheless, in many parts of the country, a more liberal attitude has become the order of the day.

One of the terms greatly emphasized by the Council was "ecumenism." The Roman body has traditionally been fenced off by a dogma which allowed no thought of a search for unity with other Churches. Indeed through the years the gap has widened with such dogmatic declarations as the Immaculate Conception of Mary and the Bodily Assumption of Mary. Vatican II did not rescind any of the existing dogmas, but did seek to make a new approach in their concern for ecumenism.

The move toward ecumenical concerns has been embraced warmly by some of the North American missionaries in Mexico. The national pastors, however do not so readily forget the persecutions suffered in the near past at the hands of those now reaching out for ecumenical dialog. Many feel that, at least in Mexico, the response to such dialog should be carefully controlled.

On the other hand it must be admitted by **everyone** that the evangelicals in Mexico have been tremendously benefitted by the new trend in the Roman Church to place the Bible in the hands of her constituents. The open Bible has opened minds and hearts of Catholics, and even the Protestants have felt the effect of this attitude.

What then should be our response to Vatican II, and what strategy should we follow in order to take advantage of unprecedented opportunities for witness? It is strikingly clear that the era of waiting in Mexico has passed. It is no longer necessary nor expedient to present a Christian witness that is less than dynamic. We must accelerate our active propagation of the Word and multiplying of churches while the climate is favorable.

C. Peter Wagner writing in *World Vision Magazine* on "Winning Roman Catholics Since Vatican II" has given five strategic suggestions for the evangelicals in Latin America (1969:20-21,24). He warns that dialogue with the Roman Catholics should be rejected because it indicates an openness to change our beliefs - something we are not willing to do. Interestingly enough, in Mexico this position has been taken by the national pastors.

Perhaps we should beware of joint discussions, debates and even prayer meetings. Do such meetings tend to be a waste of time with little possibility of winning anyone for Christ? Evangelicals need to define their objectives clearly with a concentration on the winnable Catholics. Since there are many who are searching for a Saviour, is it not good procedure to minister to these? And as conversions result, the converts should be immediately trained to witness to others with whom they have contact.

In the light of the new interest in the Bible, every effort should be made to encourage Scripture distribution and Bible reading. This kind of positive approach in an area of mutual agreement will bring more results than an emphasis on points of difference.

Protestants will continue to work and pray that each individual (man and woman, boy and girl) come to a personal knowledge of the Saviour and a conscious commitment to Him. While granting that such a commitment to Jesus Christ (not the saints, not the Virgin, not the Church, not the Pope) is possible in the Church of Rome, the Associate Reformed Presbyterians can only tell of their own commitment and open their fellowship to those who, in response to the Gospel and their election, choose to follow Christ. Each Church can win others to discipleship in itself. One Church cannot bring men to Christian commitment in another denomination. So evangelicals in Mexico in these

days of friendliness between denominations continue to urge all
men to accept Jesus Christ and continue to add all those who find
Christ through them to their branch of the Church Universal.

That the life and work of the evangelicals in Mexico have
been affected by Vatican II is unquestionable. Whether we will
convert the opportunity into real church growth remains to be
seen.

TYPE OF PERSONNEL NEEDED IN THE FUTURE

What type of missionary personnel will be needed to implement
the ministry in Mexico in the decade of the 70's? In speaking
to this problem the secretary of the Board has said:

> The Mission and the Board have not been consistent. The
> Mission says to send more missionaries and yet it seems
> there is no place for them (Gettys 1969a: Interview with
> author).

In reality the foreign personnel will depend to a great extent
upon the development of the A.R.P. Church in Mexico. We can,
however, visualize certain areas of need.

A primary need is that of evangelism. Ronnie Brunson has
written:

> I feel that if one looks at the work the A.R.P. Mission
> in Mexico is doing, they will see that the major thrust
> of our work is supervisory; yes, we all have our hand in
> evangelistic work, but in most cases it is not as a full-
> time work, only secondary and as time allows (1970: Letter
> to author).

As the national Church is at present looking towards an extended
outreach, the need arises for couples trained in evangelism who
can be free of all institutional responsibilities. With the
present distribution of the A.R.P. ministry in three states, it
might be possible to locate in each one couple dedicated to the
task of evangelism.

The School of World Mission and Institute of Church Growth
at The Fuller Theological Seminary has emphasized the importance
of nationals and North Americans totally involved in multiplying
churches. If the Church is to grow, there must be those whose
primary efforts are directed toward the goal of establishing
new congregations and nuturing them in the faith.

> Only where Christians constrained by love obediently
> press on, telling men the good news of the Savior, does
> the Church spread and increase ... Wholesome growth also
> means faithful obedience to God in developing churches so
> solid in their human matrix that they can grow, but also
> so separated and holy that they remain pleasing to God
> (McGavran 1970:15-16).

A second need would be in the field of medicine. Success in
the clinic ministry seems to depend on the use of a national
doctor. The A.R.P. Church of Mexico has among its ranks several
well qualified doctors, one of whom is at present serving in the
clinic as a missionary. This appears to be the best road to
follow. In the same connection, it is also expedient to have a
housemother for the nurses' home because the majority of the
nurses are young Christian girls from other towns and they live
in the house on the clinic grounds. Theo Kuper's ministry in
this post has been exemplary.

A third field is that of administration. The complexities
of administering and supervising have burdened missionaries who
should be given to evangelism and church planting. The question
arises: Is it not possible to have one business administrator
for the entire Mission and all the institutional work?

A fourth, somewhat nebulous field is that consisting of the
various specialities which either the national Church or the
Mission feel are necessary. In the realm of theological education, it is quite conceivable that the Church would ask for
foreign personnel as teachers. New programs under consideration by the Mexican Synod indicate a future need for specialists
in the field of Christian education. Other possibilities include music and youth work. Yet, in all of these, the ideas
and needs expressed by the national Church must for the most
part be the determining factors. It is no longer wise nor
possible for the Mission to superimpose their plans over those
of the nationals and have a harmonious ministry. And above all,
the help extended by foreign personnel in the areas of medicine
and education must not exceed the evangelistic effort. To do
so brings about a static situation and seriously curtails that
to which the missionary is dedicated - the expansion of the
Body of Christ.

What type of training should be required of those who present
themselves as candidates for the mission field? Certain basic
spiritual qualifications are essential for all. A candidate
should:
1. Be a born again Christian.
2. Be well founded in the faith of our Lord and Saviour Jesus
   Christ.

3. Have a call from God to serve in another society.
4. Rest in the grace and love of God.
5. Be available to witness in word and deed - a witness that is prompted by a burning desire to win souls.
6. Be a member of the Associate Reformed Presbyterian Church.
7. Be willing to live anywhere and serve in any capacity that his call from God dictates.

Beyond these basic spiritual requirements the well-prepared missionary candidate would do well to fulfill the following educational requirements:
1. An A. B. degree or the equivalent.
2. At least one year of Bible School or Seminary.
3. At least one year of study in a school of missions such as the School of World Mission at Fuller Theological Seminary where the focus is on attaining a sound knowledge of people, their cultures and the basic principles of cross-cultural communication of the Gospel.

In addition the candidate will find of great help the study of basic linguistic procedures such as those taught at the summer linguistic courses offered by Wycliff; the study of a variety of contemporary evangelistic methods; and the reading of periodicals relating to mission work such as *Practical Anthropology, World Vision Magazine, Evangelical Missions Quarterly, International Review of Mission* and of books such as those listed in the Bibliography. A candidate may not be able to fulfill all of these educational requirements and still meet a very real need on the mission field. He should discuss his calling with the Board to find in what capacity he can best contribute to the growth of the Church.

SUGGESTIONS FOR FUTURE CONCENTRATION

The Centennial Evangelistic Program

According to a report submitted by a joint committee (which included five missionaries, one of whom was a national, and four Mexican pastors) evangelism and church planting must take first priority in the decade we are entering. This plan has been adopted by both the Mexican Synod and the A.R.P. Mission. The Centennial Evangelistic Program has as its theme: "God's People Testifying and Teaching in God's World." Evangelism as understood by those responsible for implementing the program is:

To make Jesus Christ known to all men, in order that they accept Him as personal Saviour, receive the new life He offers, take their place in the Church, and participate in

the work of reconciliation between God and man in and for
the world (Informe Comision Mixta 1969: Translated by the
author).

Several strategic goals have been set forth:

1. That each member of the A.R.P. Church proclaim the Gospel to at least one other person each year for ten years.
2. That each church establish at least one mission church.
3. That a new congregation be established in an urban
   center each year for ten years, beginning with Mexico
   City (already established); Jalapa, Vera Cruz; Ciudad
   Victoria, Tamaulipas; and Salamanca, Guanajuato; and
   that the Presbyteries suggest the other six places.
4. That each Presbytery organize an evangelistic program
   for its own territorial needs.
5. That each Presbytery have at least one mass evangelistic
   campaign every year, either alone or in cooperation with
   other denominations, and that the campaign be planned
   in collaboration with Synod's committee.
6. That each Presbytery verify during the first year of
   this plan that enough qualified elders are working
   within the local congregations, and that during the
   second year a sufficient number of deacons are trained
   and working.
7. That a certain time be set aside each day for all
   church members to pause and pray for the evangelistic
   work throughout the Synod.
8. That radio, television, the press, etc. be utilized in
   the mass evangelistic campaigns.
9. That one evangelist dedicate his entire time to this
   ministry.
10. That a committee, consisting of one member from each
    Presbytery, two members of the Mission and the full-
    time evangelist, be named responsible to see that this
    program is faithfully carried out (Informe Comision
    Mixta 1969: Translated by the author).

Although evangelism and church planting receive the most
emphasis in the new comprehensive program elaborated by the
joint committee, a second need is also stressed. This has to
do with the teaching program of the Church. Not only must
there be an evangelistic outreach, but there must be an emphasis on nurturing the converts in the faith, as well as providing for the mature Christian growth of those already within the
fold. The administration of this phase of the plan is shown in
Plate 19.

One of the first considerations is a training program for

PLATE 19

ORGANIZATION OF THE PROGRAM OF CHRISTIAN EDUCATION
OF THE ASSOCIATE REFORMED PRESBYTERIAN CHURCH IN MEXICO

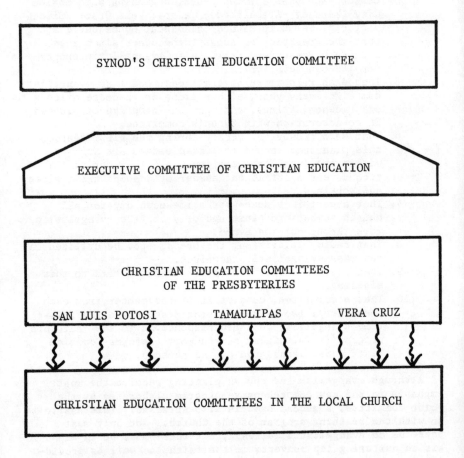

Source: Informe Comision Mixta 1969

the local leaders. It is recognized that even with excellent material and a well defined plan for the church school, little results if the teachers are untrained and irresponsible. Leadership training will be supervised by either the seminary or the executive committee of Christian education, and in the initial stages will concentrate on the pastors. Later certain pilot workshops will be held for the benefit of the entire denomination. These will be followed by training on the local level under the supervision of the minister.

Leadership training is only one facet of the implementation of the new program on the local level. Another is the organization of the local church so that all departments of the congregation might serve together in a unified manner. Then a study must be made of teaching materials available, with the aim of selecting those most relative to the A.R.P. faith and the Mexican culture and implementing their use in all the churches. Instructions for those desiring membership and baptism must be reviewed and revised. Finally, Christian stewardship must become a goal in every area of life. Each Christian as he matures in the Christian faith must be led to use his gifts of the Spirit for the benefit of God's kingdom.

It must be understood that this program is only in the blueprint stage. It is a well-thought-out plan which has many far reaching insights. Other suggestions for evangelistic and teaching campaigns in the past have failed. It is my prayer that this plan might become a reality. The possibilities for success are enlarged by the fact that it emerged from a joint committee of the Synod and the Mission rather than from only one of the two groups. That the A.R.P. Church of Mexico has vision cannot be denied. We pray that in dependence upon our God this vision might lead us to a more active outreach than at any other time in our mission history, and that it might result in a large ingathering of souls.

Strategic Geographical Areas

As seen in Plate 10, the most receptive areas for the Protestant Church in Mexico have been those near the United States and Guatemalan borders, along the Gulf Coast and in Mexico City. It would seem prudent for the A.R.P. Church which had its beginning in the gulf coast town of Tampico, to concentrate funds and personnel in this strategic gulf coast area in the decade of the 70's. This would include the coastal region of the state of Vera Cruz. From Xicotencatl, Tamaulipas, north to the Texas border, a distance of two hundred and eighty miles, the A.R.P. Church has no ministry. It would seem wise to extend our field toward the ripe fields to the north.

The urban explosion in Latin America has caused missionaries and nationals alike to look toward the cities as strategic places for establishing new churches. Mexico's urban population boomed from 5.5 million in 1930 to 17.7 million in 1960. The rural areas which have been the focal point of mission endeavor for several generations must not be abandoned. In many cases members from these small congregations form the nucleus for a new city church. However, the need for an urban ministry must not be neglected.

> While exploding urban networks present unparalleled opportunities, most churches and missions who participate in the evangelical enterprise in Latin America find themselves, like the governments in a trap, unable to move, ill prepared to redeploy men and funds into new situations (Read and Bennett 1969:11).

In looking to the future, the A.R.P. Church has selected four large cities (Mexico City, Jalapa, Ciudad Victoria and Salamanca) where churches are to be planted. Mexico City and its immediately surrounding area constitute only 15 per cent of the land area, but in this 15 per cent of the land area, 50 per cent of the population is living. The capital city is liberal and thus open to the Gospel, and the harvest is ripe. A wise measure would be to go into the other cities selected and do a preliminary survey to determine the climate or receptivity toward the Gospel before attempting to start congregations there.

The Most Responsive People

> National church leaders and missionaries must be alert to find responsive peoples, and then must concentrate their forces to reap the harvest until the last soul is brought into the Kingdom of God (Olson 1969:88).

Studies have proven that certain individuals or groups of people are often more responsive to the Gospel than others. Therefore a good policy and good stewardship for the Church is to seek out these persons and make them the object of our witness.

As regards social structure it is often the lower-class people - the majority of the population - that show the greatest receptivity. Because of their very position in society, these people long for something better, for that which will give them hope and for a light to lead them out of the darkness. Jesus Christ is the light of the world.

Within the lower class there are many homogeneous units or sub-culture groups. The immigrants and migrants, for example, because of mobility are often especially responsive. In searching for a better job, they have left the restricting pressure of their familial ties and are open for a new fellowship. Many need help in finding a place to live and in getting work. If Christian leaders could be available at this opportune time, it would greatly increase the possibilities for church planting and growth.

Those who are "down and out" are also highly receptive. They may not at first even recognize their need of a Saviour, and it is entirely probable that they may come to church for the "wrong" reasons. The story is told of a Presbyterian elder who had promised to bring at least two people to an evangelistic meeting. He forgot his responsibility until almost time for the service to begin. On remembering, he hired two men who were in need of money to go with him. At the close of the service the elder paid them their wages and bid them farewell. The following night those two men showed up, this time not under contract, with three of their friends. The elder felt obligated to pay the five because of the arrangement made the night before. However he made it quite clear that this was the last time. The end result was that two of the five were converted. It has been said in Mexico that a church can be filled at any time with a *tamale* supper and a movie. Certainly the above methods of evangelization are not advisable, but the point is that concerns people have that are secondary to a spiritual response do not necessarily prevent real response. Just as physical well-being is ultimately part of God's intention for redeemed man, so the extremities of man - even physical and psychological - are well known to be God's opportunities. When God reaches down into a human heart and that person responds with a commitment to Him, we hope that deficiencies in the method will be overshadowed by the miracle of a life made new in Christ.

These are not the only sub-cultures of people who are responsive. There are many others. The problem is to recognize such groups within our own witness area and to make a determined effort to preach the Gospel in their midst.

The Goal of an Autonomous Church

The Associate Reformed Presbyterian Church, having had missionaries in Mexico for ninety years, looks toward the centennial year of 1979 as the year when the Mexican Church will become completely autonomous. The declaration of this goal grew out of two events in the closing months of 1968. The first was the decision made at the annual meeting of the Mexican Synod to name a mixed committee of missionaries and nationals to study the possibility of making the A.R.P. Church in Mexico completely autonomous in the near future, even to the extent of controlling the institutions presently administered by missionaries. The second event occurred at the annual fall meeting of the Mission. There a motion was adopted in which the Mission formally declared its willingness to be dissolved as a Mission in 1979 when the Mexican Church would celebrate her centennial anniversary. The decision included a statement that after that time only such missionary personnel as the then-autonomous Church requested would remain.

These two actions were fused, and in 1970 the A.R.P. Church of Mexico and the Mission find themselves involved in the problems and task of realizing their united goal. The transition period will not be an easy one. Admittedly it will call for sacrifice on the part of many; it will necessitate a change of policy and a change in the way of thinking in some areas; and it will require a tremendous amount of patience and understanding.

Some problem areas are immediately evident:

Foreign Funds. Of the eighty-two preaching stations on the A.R.P. field, only nine are fully self-supporting. An additional ten congregations are being financed completely by local churches. Foreign funds are used in two areas: 1) a direct subsidy to the Mexican Synod which is used in helping support some of the churches; 2) payment of salaries of the majority of lay workers who man the preaching points. Although the economic side is not the most important aspect of the evangelistic work, it must be considered. For a Church to attain autonomy, it must be self-sufficient.

It would seem very easy and methodical to divide the subsidy which the Synod presently receives from the home Church into ten equal parts and take one away each year. At the end of ten years - presto - self support! However, it is not that simple. Other plans of decreasing the support have been tried in past years and have failed. Could every congregation continue to live through the weaning period? Would it mean that some preaching points would be abandoned? A program of tithing in the national Church does give rise to the hope that a steady decrease in the amount of the subsidy will be possible and that by the ten-year deadline there will be enough fully self-supporting churches to provide the funds for those who still require financial aid. Some feel that funds should be cut all at once rather than slowly decreasing them. Experience has shown in

many cases that such a policy is more valuable although it
seems hard at first.

Some churches are already at the point where they could sur-
vive (and probably thrive!) with all aid cut immediately. Where
this is true, it should be done. But others might need one or
two years to prepare for complete self-support. As the Synod
has prayerfully undertaken a program of stewardship and more
is expected of the individual churches and church members,
results are bound to come.

The Mission also has to get its own house in order within
the allotted time in reference to the salaries of lay workers.
This would indicate one of the following: 1)building up each
station until it is self-supporting; 2) combining two or more
stations so they can be self-sustaining; 3) phasing out the paid
worker by encouraging him to seek another way to make a living
and utilizing the non-paid lay preacher. Perhaps one, two or
all of these ideas will have to be incorporated for the transition to be successful.

At the present time the Joint Home Missions Board has under
consideration a plan for the orderly transition of all lay
workers who are under the supervision of the missionary. This
is to be done by districts, and the funds presently handled by
the missionaries will be administered by the nationals.

The ultimate withdrawal of all such funds is, of course,
the goal. The secretary of the Board of Foreign Missions in
writing the Mission concerning this matter said:

> When the Mexican Synod talks of taking over responsibility,
> this includes financial responsibility also. Personally,
> I think this does not mean an immediate cut-off of funds,
> but certainly should mean a fast cut-off (Gettys 1969b:
> Letter to Mission).

Possibly it will be better to avoid a transition during which
funds will be paid through the Mexican Synod to the lay workers.
In some parts of the world such funds have become a bone of
contention.

The missionary and the Board often fall into the fallacious
thinking that the withdrawal of support will irreparably hinder the growth of the Church and the ministry already being
carried on. That such is not necessarily the case has been
proven particularly by the Pentecostal groups who have met with
great success in some areas of Latin America.

> Self-support opens the door to unlimited expansion. One
> of the most discouraging aspects of depending on foreign
> funds for the support of pastors and churches, is that it
> automatically limits the church's capacity for expansion
> (Hodges 1953:78)

We must be confident that by working with the Mexican Church
in the goal for autonomy and self-support we are helping them
open the door to greater extension.

Scholarship Program. A big portion of the mission budget
goes toward providing scholarships for children and young
people of all ages. This part of our endeavor must also be
tested. In the final analysis everything must be put into the
balance to see if the program of scholarship aid benefits the
Church in comparison to what it costs. Is it worth spending
"x" amount of money? How does it affect church growth, numerically and depth-wise?

The Mexican Church must be consulted. Although all decisions
relating to foreign funds need the approval of the General
Synod, the Board and the Mission, the ideas of the nationals in
whose hands the responsibility will rest, must be taken into
account. We must admit that although the scholarship program
has been invaluable in providing many of our church members with
an education otherwise impossible, in fostering a trained leadership among the laymen, and in contributing to church growth,
still it might not be feasible to continue giving scholarships.
Could the present scholarship program be replaced by a scholarship loan fund administered by a committee of the Mexican Synod?

Institutions Administered by Mission. What will the emerging
Mexican Church do with the two dormitories for primary children?
Is the dormitory work important to the nationals? Will they
want to continue such a program? Can they afford to do so?
The local church already plays an important role in Colegio
Juarez, the school which the children in the dormitories attend.
It is quite conceivable that those who have been the leaders in
this educational field might be able also to administer the
dormitories financially and personnel-wise.

What about the clinic work? The clinic has been a very
worthwhile ministry and has filled a tremendous need in our
mission endeavor, our Church and the non-Christian neighborhood.
When there was no other medical service, it was a necessity.
It still will be needed for some years to come. However, with
the federal program of socialized medicine taking over more and
more territory each year, the clinic becomes less urgent as a
mission project. The possibility has been presented that by

the end of ten years the clinic would be self-supporting and
could conceivably be continued with an entire national staff
and no foreign funds. The participation of national doctors
and administrative personnel in the work of the clinic at the
present and the increasing income from patient sources make
this possibility believable.

The dispensary consumes much less foreign funds and requires
less missionary supervision than does a medical project of the
magnitude of the clinic. However, if it is to be continued,
some thought should be given as to the location. Perhaps moving
it to another rural area that presents more possibilities for
growth would be of value to the Church.

In all consideration of mission operated institutions, a
consensus of opinion of those within the national Church must
be taken into account, remembering that

> anything which hinders the development of the Church no
> matter how much immediate good it does, should be sac-
> rificed for the slower but more permanent good achieved
> through the establishment of the indigenous church
> (Hodges 1953:15).

Training of Leadership. The A.R.P. Church in Mexico and
the Mission must find a way to provide for both 1) an ordained
ministry suited to the various educational and social levels
of the people and 2) a trained lay force capable of planting
reproductive churches. In the execution of the ten year plan
for an autonomous church the first is of utmost concern.
Several years ago the Mexican Synod elected to have its own
seminary. The seminary had previously been controlled by the
Mission. The Synod elected a board of trustees to administer
funds and to select teachers. It continued to look to the
Mission for help in teaching and for provision of the major
financial apportionment. In the succeeding years this item
should be reduced in the mission budget with the understanding that the nationals would have complete control and responsibility. So far the Synod has been unable to fulfill these
responsibilities, particularly in regard to finances.

The possibility of sending the young men to one of the semi-
naries in Mexico City has been considered. This would not
seem to be the best answer, as those who live for several years
in the metropolitan area are reluctant to return to serve in
a small town or the country.

In any solution the quality of the leadership we need plays
an important part. The emphasis has been heavily scholastic

in accord with Presbyterian principles in the homeland. We do
need some Mexican Bible scholars, theologians, and translators,
but at the same time we need men trained in a good basic Bible
course who are not too far above the level of the people with
whom they work.

As we prepare them scholastically we must first and foremost
emphasize the spiritual qualifications. The requirements for
those who would attain the office of bishop (minister, presbyter,
elder, etc.) are set down in I Timothy 3:2-7(R. S. V.):

> Now a bishop must be above reproach, the husband of one
> wife, temperate, sensible, dignified, hospitable, an apt
> teacher, no drunkard, not violent but gentle, not quarrel-
> some, and no lover of money. He must manage his own house-
> hold well, keeping his children submissive and respectful
> in every way; ... He must not be a recent convert or he
> may be puffed up with conceit and fall into the condemna-
> tion of the devil; moreover he must be well thought of
> by outsiders, or he may fall into reproach and the snare
> of the devil.

Academic standards need not be thrown out, but perhaps they
need adjusting to fit the culture. It is highly possible that
in our emphasis on scholastic excellence we have overlooked
those who are eminently prepared for the ministry in the
spiritual sense. Once we focus our attention on finding men
who have the gifts of the ministry we discover that they often
have families and jobs and are unable to go off for some years
to seminary. The Guatemalan Presbyterian Church has for seven
years quite successfully given excellent training to such
people by means of an extension program. This possibility may
be seriously considered (Winter 1969).

The second problem, that of providing trained lay workers,
also suggests the idea of extension courses. With two national
ministers who are scheduled to work fulltime as itinerant super-
visors of the entire field, the suggestion becomes feasible.
Could they not arrange to have on-the-job training for individual workers and/or for groups in certain districts? Possibly
once a year a course could be given to all ministers and church
workers in a central city or village. Continuing education is
important for all church workers.

In the past, institutes have been held with a great degree
of success. These institutes could be modified for each individual presbytery or local situation and the extension course
would fit right into its proper place. In this modern era
with so much work to be done and so few to do it, the extension
system should be used to its fullest advantage.

Communication. Another problem area in the relation of the Mission to the Mexican Church has been that of communication. Now as the goal of an autonomous church is the vision of both, so must the desire to have a true sharing of ideas and decisions. Until the appointment of David and Lucia Rodriguez as missionaries, the nationals had never had a voice in the Mission. It was like two opposing worlds with the right hand not knowing what the left was doing. With the formation of a joint planning committee, lines of communication are opening up. It is no longer completely true that the missionary knows what the Church is doing, but the national still has no idea what the Mission is planning. As plans move forward, communication between the two bodies will increase. Only as it does can the transition take place. The Mexicans have a saying which quite aptly describes the solution: *Hablando se entienden las cosas.* "Things are understood by talking them over."

Only this kind of communication will allow for a responsible takeover of all phases of the work by the national. In past years the Synod (it was a presbytery under the auspices of the General Synod in the U. S. until 1964) has been governed by the Mission and the Board of Foreign Missions to a great extent. It is not my contention that this was always a bad policy. It is my belief that the time has now come to go all the way in our vote of confidence for our Mexican brothers and sisters in Christ. It has been said that they are not able to carry on the work. If we have not trusted them, are we not also saying in effect that we do not trust the Holy Spirit? We must depend on God in these days of change as never before. The nationals may not do things exactly as we do, but I am confident that they can do as well and in most cases better than we have ever done. God grant us strength to trust Him for divine guidance.

Some steps have already been taken in laying a solid foundation for an autonomous Church.

Self-Government.

The principle of self-government is so important and the result in the spiritual life of the church so vital, that if we fail here, it could well mean that we shall fail in the entire program of establishing the indigenous church (Hodges 1953:13).

In the early history the Mexican Church was largely governed by the missionary personnel. However, for some years now the nationals have been in command of the presbyteries and the Synod. The big step towards self-government came in 1964 when the *Sinodo P. A. R. de Mexico* was organized, making the Mexican

Church independent of the mother denomination. Although the ordained missionaries as members of a presbytery have a voice and
a vote, the real authority and leadership are in the hands of
the nationals.

Cooperation and availability for consultation have been the
keynote of the missionary's role in regard to government. It
is my desire that the foundation already laid be built upon as
the Mexicans continue to take more and more of the responsibility.

There should be a freedom to disagree with the Mission. This
freedom and resulting self-dependence will inevitably be fostered as the ties of monetary support are cut. At the present a
number of churches are contributing to Synod's budget in addition to meeting all their own expenses. As this number increases
and as the nationals take a firmer hold on the reins of self-
government already in their hands, real progress will be noted.

Self-Propagation. Many of the organized churches are active
in Christian outreach. Some local congregations have as many
as three missions. These are completely sustained with local
money, and leadership is provided with no salary. This is an
inspiring facet of the mission endeavor and lends real hope in
the march toward autonomy. It shows that the Mexicans have
received with joy the message of salvation and are by their
fruits proving their faith. These churches should be encouraged to continue their outreach, and as more churches become
"free agents" they should do likewise.

Vote on Return of Missionaries. A new policy of the Mission
in conjunction with the ten year plan has been to ask the Mexican Synod to vote on whether or not each missionary should return to the field following his furlough year. At the present
I believe it would be extremely difficult for the vote to be
negative because of the respect the national has always had for
the missionary and because of the inborn national trait of
courtesy. Nevertheless the door has been opened for the national
to have a voice in what foreign personnel is needed on the field.
Perhaps a further step would be to allow the Synod to make the
requisition for any new personnel and enquire if the Board can
fulfill the request.

National Missionaries. The presence of two national missionaries lends strength to the confidence that the home Board and
Synod have in the Mexicans. This should have a tremendous
effect on the relationship between the Mission and the national
Church. Congratulations go out to the Board, the Synod and the
Church at large for this big step forward and this unprecedented
insight which should continue to bring blessings for many years
in the future.

Participation of Laity. In the past the work of the Church was mainly left to the missionaries and national ministers. The general consensus of opinion was - "well they are paid for doing the work, let them do it." In recent years, especially the decade of the sixties, ordinary church members have come to the conclusion that everyone must be a witness if the Kingdom is to advance. We have seen a great "revival" in the participation of the laity. Christians are taking a more active part in the work of the Church throughout Latin America. This small beginning must be developed in order that the Church might grow at an acceptable rate.

The task ahead of us is great. The transformation will not be easy nor will it come overnight. Perhaps it will take more than the ten years we have alloted for this purpose. It will take much faith, many prayers, our complete trust in God and hard work. It will not come from contemplation, but with much sweat and many tears. Let us not look back. We must press forward with our eyes fixed on Him who is able to keep us from falling.

Will you not pray for our emerging Mexican Church, earnestly desiring that the Holy Spirit would move not only there, but in the homeland, in Pakistan and throughout the entire world?

Ministry Among the Indians

The section dealing with the history of Mexico presented a graphic description of the mosaic of Indian civilization at the time of the Spanish conquest. Few people realize that at the present time approximately 20 per cent of the populace is composed of pure-blood Indians. Eighty-eight different languages are still spoken among these people, although Spanish is the official tongue of the country. The early venture of two of our missionaries in beginning a ministry among the Indians has been noted. That work became a separate mission in the 40's. Since that time the A.R.P. Church has attempted to minister to a small portion of the Indian populace within the bounds of our denomination. There are twelve congregations with a communicant membership of two hundred fifteen. The homogeneous groupings of the Indian tribes offer an area of high potential for church growth. The question arises then as to why we have neglected this fruitful segment of the population, and what has caused our failure to show real results there.

First it must be understood that the Indians are an animistic people. Animism is technically defined as a "belief in spirits, including the spirits of dead people as well as those that have no human origin' (Nida and Smalley 1959:5). However,

a broader understanding includes all types of primitive re-
ligions which are not an orthodox part of the world's major
faiths.

In Mexico where Roman Catholicism is the majority religion
of the land, animism may not be the primary or at least the
official form of belief, but the beliefs of the common people
and most especially of the Indians are essentially animistic.
Several examples illustrate the point..

The Mazatec people always speak of a child as being ugly so
as to fool the malicious spirits whom they carefully refer to
as "good spirits." For the Huichol Indians, healing and religion go together and for religious instruction to be accepted
it must be given by the medicine man known as a *curandero*. The
Chols in southern Mexico believe that the devil heads up the
world of man. He must be appeased at any cost. They also link
other ills with the world of spirits. The spirit of the frog
supposedly causes bloated stomachs, the spirit of wasps inflicts
boils and the spirit of the mole produces toothaches. Certain
of the Aztecs, although acknowledging God as the creator deity,
still retain the ancient concept of multiple creations and de-
structions of the world. The curious power and influence of
the *curandero* was mentioned by Dr. Dale on beginning his ministry among the Indians.

> Those medicine men practice their cures in line with the
> current ideas of the Indians. The latter believe that when
> a person dies his soul does not leave this world at all.
> It enters a tree, stone, or animal, and from time to time,
> takes vengeance on the living ... To the Indians, there-
> fore, not bacteria but these evil spirits cause sickness
> ... He (the medicine man) is the only person thought to
> be capable of communicating with and appeasing these angry
> spirits (Dale 1943:114).

In attempting to work among the Indians we have largely ig-
nored these animistic tendencies glossed over by a superficial
allegiance to Roman Catholicism. In understanding then what the
Indian is and what he believes, the task of how to confront him
with the Gospel is clarified. The Indians have responded
notably to an emphasis on the love of God. Christian concepts
can best be taught by the biblical method of showing how these
principles apply to definite situations. All material should
be made relevant to the specific beliefs and practices of the
Indian group. There must be found, if at all possible, some
functional substitutes for the objectionable animistic features.
And above all, the missionary, minister or lay worker must witness to the Indian in his "heart language" rather than relying

on interpreters or using Spanish which is spoken by only some.

What does all of this say to the A.R.P. Church? It points out a need for renewed concentration in our efforts to evangelize the Indians. It suggests the use of well prepared lay workers in this field. It calls for a clear understanding of the animistic beliefs in the tribes to be evangelized. And finally, in recognition of the Indian personality and homogeneity, it implies the establishment of a new presbytery composed entirely of Indian congregations where there will be no sense of competition with the mestizos and possible rejection by them.

CONCLUSION

This case study of the development of the Associate Reformed Presbyterian Church in Mexico has traced the emergence of a Church through the ninety years of its history. It has raised questions in my mind in many instances and has produced a deeper insight into the form and shape of our mission work there. It has given me cause for thanksgiving in some cases and brought deep sighs of regret in others. It is presented with the prayerful desire that it will cause all to take a new look at what has happened and seriously evaluate the present and future of our mission endeavor in Mexico.

APPENDIX

A   ASSOCIATE REFORMED PRESBYTERIAN CONGREGATIONS IN MEXICO,
1970: COMMUNICANT MEMBERSHIP, SYMPATHIZERS AND STATUS

B   ADDRESSES OF INTERDENOMINATIONAL SOCIETIES WORKING IN
MEXICO

APPENDIX A

ASSOCIATE REFORMED PRESBYTERIAN CONGREGATIONS IN MEXICO 1970
COMMUNICANT MEMBERSHIP, SYMPATHIZERS AND STATUS

SAN LUIS POTOSI	TAMAULIPAS	VERA CRUZ	MEMBERS	SYMPATHIZERS	CHURCH	MISSION
Agualitla			15	45		C
Amaynac			5	15		C
	Ant. Morelos		50	80	x	
	Arbol Grande		47	64	x	
Ayotosco			20	30		C
Canada Grande			3	40		H
Cardenas			150	71	x	
Cerrito de la Cruz			10	80		H
Cerritos			8	30		H
		Cerro Azul	15	30	x	
Ciudad del Maiz			60	45	x	

Notes:
1. Sympathizers include unbaptized adults who attend services and children.
2. Church indicates an organized congregation.
3. Mission includes preaching points supported by local congregations (indicated by name of supporting church) and those under the supervision of the Home Mission Board. The initials indicate the missionary (C – Covone, H – Halliday, W – Whitesides) who directly oversees the work and pays the lay worker.

SAN LUIS POTOSI	TAMAULIPAS	VERA CRUZ	MEMBERS	SYMPATHIZERS	CHURCH	MISSION
	Ciudad Madero		250	185	x	
	Ciudad Mante		180	145	x	
Ciudad Valles			120	130	x	
		Col. Bermudez	50	45		W
Col. El Meco			14	30	x	
	Col. M. Aleman			30		Mante
	Col. Tamaulipas					W
	Col. Vergel		30	46	x	
		Corral Viejo	8	11		W
Ebano			12	23		W
	El Abra		20	26		Quintero
El Canon			40	55	x	
	El Limon		2	17		Xicotencatl
		El Naranjo	10	25		W
El Platanito			15	14		C
El Progreso			9	20		H
	Ejido Cuauhtemoc		8	35		Mante
	Ejido El Potosi		5	22		Mante

SAN LUIS POTOSI	TAMAULIPAS	VERA CRUZ	MEMBERS	SYMPATHIZERS	CHURCH	MISSION
	Ejido El Siete			17		San Rafael
	Estacion Colonia		6	44		W
		Estanzuela	46	57		W
Ixtacamel			22	39		C
		Kilometro 12	5	15		Tuxpam
Labor Vieja			18	50		H
Lagunillas			5	15		H
La Loma				18		C
La Pagua			10	30		C
La Pimienta			60	50	x	C
La Union				50		C
	Las Flores		6	30		C
Las Palmas			13	30		C
	Lomas del Real		16	25	x	W
	Los Aztecas			35		W
	Los Esteros		17	39		W
	Manuel		2	30		W
		Magozal	12	39		W

SAN LUIS POTOSI	TAMAULIPAS	VERA CRUZ	MEMBERS	SYMPATHIZERS	CHURCH	MISSION
Naranjito				10		Rayon
Nueva Angostura			20	20		H
		Ozuluama		37		W
		Panuco	45	33	x	C
Petlacoyo			20	38		
		Poza Rica	73	80	x	
Providencia				30		H
		Quebrache	32	23		W
Quinta Mercedes			4			San L. P.
	Quintero		40	38	x	
	Rancho Nuevo		17	27	x	
		Rancho Nuevo	15	21		W
Rascon			8	45		C
Rayon			16	40		H
Rioverde			143	93	x	
Sabino, Coxcatlan			5	20		C
San Bartolo			8	25		H
San Luis Potosi			35	34	x	
San Pedro						C

SAN LUIS POTOSI	TAMAULIPAS	VERA CRUZ	MEMBERS	SYMPATHIZERS	CHURCH	MISSION
	San Rafael		17	35	x	C
Soledad			15	30		C
Tamasopo			20	52		C
Tamazunchale			22	39	x	
	Tampico		106	205	x	
	Tampico Mission		30	60		Tampico
Tamuin			15	30	x	
		Tantima	25	60		W
		Tantoyuca	10	39		W
		Tihuatlan	5	15		
Tlacuapa			8	22		C
		Tuxpam	160	97	x	
		V. Naranjos	8	18		W
	Xicotencatl		43	31	x	
TOTALS 39	24	17				

DISTRITO FEDERAL

Mexico City			20	15	x	

GUANAJUATO

Salamanca			10	15		
TOTALS 82			2,389	3,349	26	56

ADDRESSES OF INTERDENOMINATIONAL SOCIETIES WORKING IN MEXICO

Air Mail From God Mission, Inc.
(Now called Trans-World Missions)
4205 Santa Monica Blvd.
Los Angeles, California 90029

American Bible Society
1865 Broadway
New York, New York 10023

Back Country Evangelism, Inc.
Apdo. 45
Cuatla, Morelos MEXICO

Campus Crusade for Christ, Inc.
Arrowhead Springs
San Bernadino, California 92403

Evangelical Foreign Missions Association
100 Western Union Building
1405 G Street, N. W.
Washington, D. C. 20005

Gospel Films, Inc.
Box 455
Muskegon, Michigan 49443

Gospel Missionary Union
Smithville, Missouri 64089

Gospel Recordings, Inc.
122 Glendale Blvd.
Los Angeles, California 90026

Greater Mexican Missions, Inc.
1911 South 48th
Lincoln, Nebraska 68506

Harvesters International Mission, Inc.
Box 1986
McAllen, Texas 78501

Heifer Project, Inc.
202 West Main Street
Box 269
North Manchester, Indiana 46962

Interdenominational Foreign Mission Association
54 Bergen Ave.
Ridgefield Park, New Jersey 07660

Laubach Literacy Fund, Inc.
Box 131
Syracuse, New York 13210

Mexican Militant Mission, Inc.
Box 636
Pharr, Texas 78577

Missionary Aviation Fellowship
Box 32
Fullerton, California 92632

Missionary and Soul Winning Fellowship
Box 7271
Long Beach, California 90807

Overseas Crusades, Inc.
265 Lytton Ave.
Palo Alto, California 94301

Practical Missionary Training, Inc.
Box 628
Fullerton, California 92632

Scripture Gift Mission   (American Scripture Gift Mission)
Radstock House   441 Bourse Building
London, England   Philadelphia, Pennsylvania 19106

Short-Term Abroad
129 North Main Street
Wheaton, Illinois 60187

Spanish World Gospel Broadcasting, Inc.
Box 335
Winona Lake, Indiana

The Gideons International
2900 Lebanon Road
Nashville, Tennessee 37214

The Navigators, Inc.
Box 1659
Colorado Springs, Colorado 80901

The Pocket Testament League, Inc.
49 Honeck Street
Englewood, New Jersey 07631

World Gospel Mission
123 West Fifth Street
Marion, Indiana 46952

World Literature Crusade
Box 1313
Studio City, California 91604

World Missions, Inc.
3759 Atlantic Avenue
Box 2611
Long Beach, California

World Vision International
919 West Huntington Drive
Monrovia, California 91016

World-Wide Mission
1593 East Colorado Blvd.
Box G
Pasadena, California 91109

Wycliffe Bible Translators, Inc.
219 West Walnut
Box 1960
Santa Ana, California 92702

Youth Enterprises, Inc.
Box 1001
Imperial Beach, California 92032

G L O S S A R Y

Acta Constitutiva	Organizational charter.
Amigos de Jesus	Friends of Jesus.
A. R. P.	Associate Reformed Presbyterian.
Cantos Biblicos	Bible Songs, the official song book of the Associate Reformed Presbyterian Church of Mexico.
Church	The Church universal, a denomination, or a proper name.
church	A building, a local congregation or an adjective.
Ciudad	City.
Colonia	A colony; a district or suburb of the city.
Conquistadores	Conquerors.
Diaconisa	Deaconess, director of Christian education.
Ejido	Communal farm.
Ejidatario	Communal farmer.
Esfuerzo Cristiano	Young People's Christian Union.
Evangelical	Protestant Christian.
Iglesia Presbiteriana Asociada Reformada Principe de Paz	Prince of Peace Associate Reformed Presbyterian Church.
Junta Unida de Misiones Domesticas	United Home Missions Board.
Los Estados Unidos Mexicanos	The United Mexican States; Mexico.

Mestizo	A ladino; a person of mixed blood.
Mission	The mission board or society of a foreign Church or the mission organization within a country.
mission	A preaching point which is not an organized church or an adjective.
Plaza	Main square of a Mexican town.
Rancho	Ranch.
Sinodo Presbiteriano Asociado Reformado de Mexico	Associate Reformed Presbyterian Synod of Mexico.
Sociedad Femenil	Woman's Society.
Sympathizer	One who is in sympathy with the Protestant movement although not a baptized believer.
Tierra caliente	Hot country.

BIBLIOGRAPHY

ALLEN, Roland
1962   *Missionary Methods: St. Paul's or Ours?* Grand Rapids,
        Wm. B. Eerdmans Publishing Co.

ASCHMANN, Homer, BRANDERBURG, Frank, BROTHERS, Dwight and QUIRK,
Robert
1970   "Mexico," Chicago, *World Book Encyclopedia*. Vol. 13:
        372-388.

ASSOCIATE REFORMED PRESBYTERIAN CHURCH
1879-1969 *Minutes of the General Synod of the Associate
        Reformed Presbyterian Church.*

ASSOCIATE REFORMED PRESBYTERIAN MISSION
1968-1969 General Minutes.

BAEZ CAMARGO, Gonzalo and GRUBB, Kenneth G.
1935   *Religion in the Republic of Mexico.* New York, World
        Dominion Press.

BARNETT, H. G.
1953   *Innovation: The Basis of Cultural Change.* New York,
        McGraw-Hill Book Co., Inc.

BENNETT, Charles
1968   *Tinder in Tabasco.* Grand Rapids, Wm. B. Eerdmans Pub-
        lishing Co.

BERKOUWER, G. C.
1965   *The Second Vatican Council and the New Catholicism.*
        Grand Rapids, Wm. B. Eerdmans Publishing Co. (Trans-
        lated by Lewis B. Smedes from the original Dutch.)

BOJORQUEZ, Juan de Dios, ed.
1932   *Memoria de los Census Generales de Poblacion Agricola
        Ganadero e Industrial.* Mexico, D. F. Departamento de
        la Estadistica Nacional.

BOYCE, W. W.
1969   Interview with author, December 17, 1969.

BRADEN, Charles S.
    1930   *Religious Aspects of the Conquest of Mexico.* Durham,
           N. C., Duke University Press.

BRAWLEY, Robert L.
    1970   Letter to author, January 30, 1970.

BRODERICK, J. F.
    1967   "Jesuits," New York, *New Catholic Encyclopedia.*
           Vol. 7:898-909.

BRUNSON, R. L.
    1970   Letter to author, February 15, 1970.

BUKER, Raymond C., Sr.
    1964   "Missionary Encounter With Culture," *Evangelical
           Missions Quarterly,* 1:9-18.

BURLAND, C. A.
    1967   *The Gods of Mexico.* London, Eyre and Spottiswoods.

CASO, Antonio
    1955   *El Problema de Mexico.* Mexico, D. F., Ediciones
           Libro-Mex.

CASTANEDA, Ruben
    1969   Letter to author, November 11, 1969.

CLINE, Howard F.
    1962a "Mexico," Chicago, *Encyclopedia Brittanica.* Vol. 15:
           377-396.

    1962b *Mexico: Revolution to Evolution.* London, Oxford Uni-
           versity Press.

CONSIDINE, John J., ed.
    1966   *The Religious Dimension in the New Latin America.*
           Notre Dame, Ind., Fides Publishers, Inc.

CORWIN, Arthur F.
    1963   *Contemporary Mexican Attitudes Toward Population,
           Poverty, and Public Opinion.* Jacksonville, Fla., The
           N. and W. B. Drew Company.

COVONE, Imogene
    1961   "A Strength to the Needy in His Distress," *The Synodi-
           cal Journal,* (February) 4.

COVONE, Imogene
1967 "Neill E. Pressly Clinic," *The Synodical Journal,*
(February) 3.

COVONE, P. G.
1969 Letter to author, December 5, 1969.

COWAN, Marion M.
1962 "A Christian Movement in Mexico," *Practical Anthropology,* 9:193-204.

CUMBERLAND, Charles C.
1968 *Mexico: The Struggle for Modernity.* New York, Oxford
University Press.

DALE, James G.
1910 *Mexico and Our Mission.* Lebanon, Pa., Press of Sowers
Printing Company.

1943 *Katherine Neel Dale: Medical Missionary.* Grand Rapids,
Wm. B. Eerdmans Publishing Co.

DALE, John T.
1969 Letter to author, November 26, 1969.

ELLISON, John W., ed.
1957 *Nelson's Complete Concordance of the Revised Standard
Version.* New York, Thomas Nelson and Sons.

EWING, Russel C., ed.
1967 *Six Faces of Mexico.* Tuscon, Arizona, The University
of Arizona Press.

FAGG, John Edwin
1963 *Latin America: A General History.* New York, Macmillan
Co.

FARRISS, N. M.
1968 *Crown and Clergy in Colonial Mexico.* London, The
Atholone Press, University of London.

GALLEGOS, Alejandro
n. d. "Notas Sobre La Historia de la Iglesia Presbiteriana
'Principe de Paz' de Cd. Mante, Tamps." A history
prepared for the tenth anniversary of the church.
(Mimeographed.)

GALLOWAY, J. C., ed.
 1905   *The Centennial History of the Associate Reformed Pres-
        byterian Church*. Charleston, S. C., Press of Walker,
        Evans and Cogswell Co.

GARIBAY, A. M.
 1967   "Our Lady of Guadalupe," New York, *New Catholic En-
        cyclopedia*. Vol. 6:821-822.

GETTYS, E.
 1969a Interview with author, December 17, 1969.

 1969b Letter to Mission, November 5, 1969.

GIBSON, John M.
 1958   *Soldiers of the Word: The Story of the American Bible
        Society*. New York, Philosophical Library, Inc.

GLEASON GALICIA, Ruben, ed.
 1968   *Revista de Estadistica*, Mexico, D. F., Talleres
        Graficos de la Nacion. (junio).

GRIFFIN, William B.
 1969   *Culture Change and Shifting Populations in Central
        Northern Mexico*. Tuscon, The University of Arizona
        Press.

GRUENING, Ernest
 1940   *Mexico and Its Heritage*. New York, D. Appleton-Century
        Co.

GUAY, Viola
 1970   "Land Tenure in Mexico," *Mexican World*, (January)
        10-11.

HALLIDAY, Flora Harper
 1969   Letter to author.

HALLIDAY, W. C.
 1951   *Mexico Looks Up*. Rio Verde, S.L.P., Mexico, Ediciones
        Par.

 1969-1970 Private Correspondence.

HARING, Bernard
 1966   *Road to Renewal*. Staten Island, N. Y., Alba House.

HASTINGS, Adrian
 1967 *Church and Mission in Modern Africa.* Bronx, New York, Fordham University Press.

HINNESBUSCH, W. A.
 1967 "Dominican Spirituality," New York, *New Catholic Encyclopedia.* Vol. 6:38-46.

HODGES, Melvin L.
 1953 *The Indigenous Church.* Springfield, Missouri, The Gospel Publishing House.

INFORME COMISION MIXTA
 1969 A report prepared by a joint committee of missionaries and national pastors and approved by the Mexican Synod and the A.R.P. Mission. (Mimeographed.)

ISAIS, Juan M.
 1966 *The Other Side of the Coin.* Grand Rapids, Wm. B. Eerdmans Publishing Co.

JUAREZ, Ascencion
 1970 Letter to author, March 12, 1970.

KANE, J. Herbert
 1956 *Faith, Mighty Faith.* New York, Interdenominational Foreign Mission Association.

KENNEDY, W. A., ed.
 1951 *The Sesquicentennial History of Associate Reformed Presbyterian Church.* Clinton, S. C., Presses of Jacobs Brothers Printers.

LATOURETTE, Kenneth Scott
 1953 *A History of Christianity.* New York, Harper and Row.

LESLIE, Ruth R.
 1923 "The Protestant Movement in Mexico." An unpublished M. A. dissertation, College of Missions.

LEWIS, Oscar
 1959 *Five Families: Mexican Case Studies in the Culture of Poverty.* New York, Basic Books Inc.

 1960 *Tepoztlan Village in Mexico.* New York, Holt, Rinehart and Winston, Inc.

 1961 *The Children of Sanchez.* New York, Random House.

LOPEZ, Maurilio
   1970   Letter to author, February 24, 1970.

MCCLELLAND, Alice J.
   1960   *Mission to Mexico*. Nashville, Tenn., The Board of
          World Missions, Presbyterian Church, U. S.

MCELROY, RACHEL
   1969   Letter to author, December 9, 1969.

MCGAVRAN, Donald A.
   1962   *Church Growth in Jamaica*. Lucknow, U. P., India,
          Lucknow Publishing House.

   1963   *Church Growth in Mexico*. Grand Rapids, Wm. B. Eerd-
          mans Publishing Co.

   1965a "Introduction" in Read 1965.

   ed.
   1965b *Church Growth and Christian Mission*. New York, Harper
          and Row.

   1966   *How Churches Grow*. New York, Friendship Press.

   1968   *Bridges of God*. New York, Friendship Press.

   ed.
   1969a *Church Growth Bulletin*. Volumes I - V. South Pasadena,
          California, William Carey Library.

   ed.
   1969b *Church Growth Bulletin*. Vol. VI, No. 2, Pasadena,
          California, Fuller Theological Seminary.

   1970   *Understanding Church Growth*. Grand Rapids, Wm. B.
          Eerdmans Publishing Co.

MADSEN, William
   1964   *The Mexican-Americans of South Texas*. New York, Holt,
          Rinehart and Winston.

MATTHEWS, Basil
   1960   *Forward Through the Ages*. New York, Friendship Press.

MEDARY, Marjorie
   1966   *Each One Teach One: Frank Laubach, Friend to Millions*.
          New York, David McKay Company, Inc.

MISSIONARY RESEARCH LIBRARY
  1968   *North American Protestant Ministries Overseas.* Waco,
         Texas, Word Books.

MONROY RIVERA, Oscar
  1966   *El Mexicano Enano.* Mexico, D. F., B. Costa-Amic.

MOSES, Jasper T.
  1903   *Today in the Land of Tomorrow.* Indianapolis, The
         Christian Woman's Board of Mission.

NEILL, Stephen
  1964   *A History of Christian Missions.* Harmondsworth,
         Middlesex, England, Penguin Books.

NELSON, Claud D.
  1962   *The Vatican Council and All Christians.* New York,
         Association Press.

NIDA, Eugene A.
  1954   *Customs and Cultures.* New York, Harper and Row.

  1960   *Message and Mission.* New York, Harper and Row.

  1967   "The Relationship of Social Structures to the Problems
         of Evangelism in Latin America" in Wm. A. Smalley (ed.)

NIDA, Eugene and SMALLEY Wm. A.
  1959   *Introducing Animism.* New York, Friendship Press.

NUNEZ, Theron Aldine, Jr.
  1963   "Cultural Discontinuity and Conflict in a Mexican
         Village." An unpublished Ph. D. dissertation, Uni-
         versity of California, Berkley. (m/f used)

OLMEDO, D.
  1967   "Mexico, Colonial," New York, *New Catholic Encyclo-
         pedia.* Vo. 9:770-775.

OLSON, Gilbert W.
  1969   *Church Growth in Sierra Leone.* Grand Rapids, Wm. B.
         Eerdmans Publishing Co.

PARKS, Henry Banford
  1960   *A History of Mexico.* Boston, Houghton Mifflin Co.

PATTERSON, Andrew M.
  1967   "Mexico," New York, *Worldmark Encyclopedia of the
         Nations.* Vol. 3:181-194.

PESINA GONZALEZ, Amador
1969-1970 Private Correspondence.

POZAS, Ricardo
    1966   *Juan the Chamula*. Berkley, California, University of
           California Press. (Translated by Lysander Kemp from
           the original Spanish.)

RAMOS, Rutilio, ALONSO, Isidore and GARRE, Domingo
    1963   *La Iglesia en Mexico*. Bogota, Colombia, Oficina Inter-
           nacional de Investigaciones Sociales de FERES.

READ, William
    1965   *New Patterns of Church Growth in Brazil*. Grand Rapids,
           Wm. B. Eerdmans Publishing Co.

READ, William and BENNETT, Charles
    1969   "Urban Explosion: The Challenge in Latin America,"
           World Vision Magazine, (June) 6-11.

READ, William, MONTERROSO, Victor M. and JOHNSON, Harmon A.
    1969   *Latin American Church Growth*. Grand Rapids, Wm. B.
           Eerdmans Publishing Co.

RICARD, Robert
    1966   *The Spiritual Conquest of Mexico*. Berkley, California,
           University of California Press. (Translated by Lesley
           B. Simpson from the original French.)

RIVERA, Pedro
    1962   *Instituciones Protestantes En Mexico*. Mexico, D. F.
           Editorial Jus S. A.

ROBERTS, C. Paul, ed.
    1968   *Statistical Abstract of Latin America 1967*. Los
           Angeles, Latin American Center.

RUIZ, Ramon Eduardo
    1963   *Mexico: The Challenge of Poverty and Illiteracy*. San
           Marino, California, The Huntington Library.

SCHLINK, Edmund
    1968   *After the Council*. Philadelphia, Fortress Press.
           (Translated by Herbert J. A. Bouman from the original
           German.)

SCHWARTZ, Lola Romancicci Manzolillo
  1962   "Morality, Conflict and Violence in a Mexican Mestizo
        Village." An unpublished Ph. D. dissertation, Indiana
        University. (m/f used)

SHANNON, A. C.
  1967   "Augustinians," New York, *New Catholic Encyclopedia.*
        Vol. 1:1071-1076.

SHEARER, Roy E.
  1966   *Wildfire: Church Growth in Korea.* Grand Rapids, Wm.
        B. Eerdmans Publishing Co.

SIMPSON, Lesley Byrd
  1961   *Many Mexicos.* Berkley, California, University of
        California Press.

SMALLEY, William A., ed.
  1967   *Readings in Missionary Anthropology.* Tarrytown, New
        York, Practical Anthropology, Inc.

TAVARD, George H.
  1965   *The Church Tomorrow.* New York, Herder and Herder.

TAYLOR, Clyde W. and COGGINS, Wade T., eds.
  1961   *Protestant Missions in Latin America: A Statistical
        Survey.* Washington, D. C., Evangelical Foreign
        Missions Association.

THOMPSON, J. Eric S.
  1966   *The Rise and Fall of the Maya Civilization.* Norman,
        University of Oklahoma Press.

THOMPSON, Phyliss
  1962   *Faith by Hearing.* Los Angeles, Gospel Recordings Inc.

TIPPETT, A. R.
  1966   "Church Growth or Else!" *World Vision Magazine,*
        (February) 12-13, 28.

  1969   *Verdict Theology in Missionary Theory.* Lincoln,
        Illinois, Lincoln Christian College Press.

WAGNER, C. Peter
  1969   "Winning Roman Catholics (Since Vatican II)," *World
        Vision Magazine,* (April) 20-21, 24.

WESTBURG, Paul A.
   1959   *They Stood Every Man in His Place*.   Chicago, The
           Gideons International.

WESTLUND, Lester P.
   1968   "Avoiding the Dangers of Mission Institutions,"
           Evangelical Missions Quarterly, Vol. 4:231-234.

WHITESIDES, Harriett Lou
   1967   "The Mexican Church Coming of Age," *The Synodical
           Journal*, (April) 13-14.

   1969   Letter to author, November 26, 1969.

WHITESIDES, Robert A.
   1967   *Christ Builds His Church in Mexico*.   Charlotte, North
           Carolina, Associated Publishers, Inc.

   1969   Letter to author, November 27, 1969.

WINTER, Ralph D., ed.
   1969   *Theological Education by Extension*.   South Pasadena,
           California, William Carey Library.

WOLD, Joseph Conrad
   1968   *God's Impatience in Liberia*.   Grand Rapids, Wm. B.
           Eerdmans Publishing Co.

ZERTUCHE CARRILLO, Albino, ed.
   1963   *Anuario Estadística de los Estados Unidos Mexicanos*.
           Mexico, D. F. Talleres Graficos de la Nacion.

INDEX

William Carey Library

Publications

533 HERMOSA STREET
SOUTH PASADENA, CALIFORNIA 91030

Theological Education by Extension, edited by Ralph D.
Winter, Ph.D.
  A husky handbook on a new approach to the education
of pastoral leadership for the church. Gives both theory
and practice and the exciting historical development of
the "largest non-governmental voluntary educational
development project in the world today." -Ted Ward, Pro-
fessor of Education, Michigan State University.
  1969: 648 pages, Library Buckram $7.95, Kivar $4.95.
  ISBN 0-87808-101-1

Peoples of Southwest Ethiopia, by Alan R. Tippett, Ph.D.
  A recent, penetrating evaluation by a professional
anthropologist of the cultural complexities faced by
Peace Corps workers and missionaries in a rapidly
changing intersection of African states.
  1970: 304 pages, Softbound, $3.95. ISBN 0-87808-103-8

*The Church of the United Brethren in Christ in Sierra
Leone,* by Emmett D. Cox, Executive Secretary, United
Brethren in Christ Board of Missions.
  A readable account of the relevant historical, demo-
graphic and anthropological data as they relate to the
development of the United Brethren in Christ Church in
the Mende and Creole communities. Includes a reforma-
tion of objectives.
  1970: 184 pages, Softbound, $2.95. ISBN 0-87808-301-4

The Christian Advance in Indonesia, by Ebbie C. Smith, Th.D.
  The fascinating details of the penetration of Christianity into the Indonesian archipelago make for intensely
interesting reading, as the anthropological context and
the growth of the Christian movement are highlighted.
  1970: 216 pages, Softbound, $3.45. ISBN 0-87808-302-2

The Twenty-Five Unbelievable Years: 1945-1969, by Ralph D. Winter, Ph.D.

A terse, exciting analysis of the most significant transition in human history in this millenium and its impact upon the Christian movement. "Packed with insight and otherwise unobtainable statistical data...a brilliant piece of work." -C. Peter Wagner.

1970: 116 pages, Softbound $1.95. ISBN 0-87808-102-X

The Emergence of a Mexican Church: The Associate Reformed Presbyterian Church of Mexico, by James Erskine Mitchell.

Tells the ninety-year story of the Associate Reformed Presbyterian mission in Mexico, the trials and hardships as well as the bright side of the work. Eminently practical and helpful regarding the changing relationship of mission and church in the next decade.

1970: 192 pages, Softbound, $2.95. ISBN 0-87808-303-0

The Young Life Campaign and the Church, by Warren Simandle.

If 70 per cent of young people drop out of the church between the ages of 12 and 20, is there room for a nation-wide Christian organization working on high school campuses? After a quarter of a century, what is the record of Young Life and how has its work with teens affected the church? "A careful analysis based on a statistical survey; full of insight and challenging proposals for both Young Life and the church."

1970: 216 pages, Softbound, $3.45. ISBN 0-87808-304-9

Church Growth Through Evangelism-in-Depth, by Malcolm R. Bradshaw.

"Examines the history of Evangelism-in-Depth and other total mobilization approaches to evangelism. Also presents concisely the 'Church Growth' approach to mission and proposes a wedding between the two...a great blessing to the church at work in the world." *World Vision Magazine*.

1969: 152 pages, Softbound, $2.45. ISBN 0-87808-401-0

The Protestant Movement in Bolivia, by C. Peter Wagner.

An excitingly-told account of the gradual build-up and present vitality of Protestantism. A cogent analysis of the various sub-cultures and the organizations working most effectively, including a striking evaluation of Bolivia's momentous Evangelism-in Depth year and the possibilities of Evangelism-in-Depth for other parts of the world.

1970: 264 pages, Softbound, $3.95. ISBN 0-87808-402-9

Profile for Victory in Zambia, by Max Ward Randall.
  "In a remarkably objective manner the author has analyzed
contemporary political, social, educational and religious
trends which demand a re-examination of traditional missionary methods and the creation of daring new strategies...his
conclusions constitute a challenge for the future of Christian missions, not only in Zambia, but around the world."
                                        -James DeForest Murch
  1970: 224 pages, Cloth, $3.95. ISBN 0-8708-403-7

*Taiwan: Mainline Versus Independent Church Growth, A Study
in Contrasts,* by Allen J. Swanson.
  A provocative comparison between the older, historical
Protestant churches in Taiwan and the new indigenous Chinese
churches; suggests staggering implications for missions everywhere that intend to promote the development of truly indigenous expressions of Christianity.
  1970: 216 pages, Softbound, $2.95. ISBN 0-87808-404-5

The Church Growth Bulletin, Volumes I-V, edited by Donald A.
McGavran, Ph.D.
  The first five years of issues of a now-famous bulletin
which probes past foibles and present opportunities facing
the 100,000 Protestant and Catholic missionaries in the
world today. No periodical edited for this audience has a
larger readership.
  1969: 408 pages, Library Buckram $6.95, Kivar $4.45.
  ISBN 0-87808-701-X

El Seminario de Extension: Un Manual, by James H. Emery, F.
Ross Kinsler, Ralph D. Winter, Louise J. Walker.
  Gives the reasons for the extension approach to the training of ministers, as well as the concrete, practical details
of establishing and operating such a program. A Spanish
translation of the third section of *Theological Education by
Extension*.
  1969: 256 pages, Softbound, $3.45. ISBN 0-87808-801-6

Note: You may order by using the last four digits of the
ISBN numbers, e.g. 801-6 is the book just above. Five or
more books receive a 20% discount, ten or more are 40% off.
But please send 30 cents per book on all orders to cover
postage and handling. (Bookstores are not charged for
handling and are billed for the exact amount of postage.
Same discount rate.) California residents must add 5%
sales tax.

ABOUT THE WILLIAM CAREY LIBRARY

William Carey is widely considered the "Father of Modern Missions" partly because many people think he was the first Protestant missionary. Even though there was a trickle of others before him, he deserves very special honor for many valiant accomplishments in his heroic career, but most particularly because of three things he did before he ever left England, things no one else in history before him had combined together:

1) he had an authentic, personal, evangelical passion to serve God and acknowledged this as obligating him to fulfill God's interests in the redemption of all men on the face of the earth,

2) he actually proposed a structure for the accomplishment of that aim - he did indeed, more than anyone else, set off the movement among Protestants for the creation of "voluntary societies" for foreign missions, and

3) he added to all of this a strategic literary and research achievement: shaky those statistics may have been, but he put together the very best possible estimate of the number of unreached peoples in every part of the globe, and summarized previous, relatively ineffective attempts to reach them. His burning conclusion was that existing efforts were not proportional to the opportunities and the scope of Christian obligation in Mission.

Today, a little over 150 years later, the situation is not wholly different. In the past five years, for example, experienced missionaries from all corners of the earth (53 countries) have brought to the Fuller School of World Mission and Institute of Church Growth well over 800 years of missionary experience. Twenty-six scholarly books have resulted from the research of faculty and students. The best statistics available have at times been shaky -though far superior to Carey's - but vision has been clear and the mandate is as urgent as ever. Other schools and scholars are giving more attention to the Christian Mission. Carey proposed an international meeting of missionaries every ten years to facilitate the fulfillment of the Great Commission, but far more people read his statistical analysis of the needs and opportunities than ever got together in one place. The printing press is still the right arm of Christians active in the Christian world mission.

The William Carey Library is a new publishing house dedicated to books related to this mission. There are many publishers, both secular and religious, that occasionally publish books of this kind. We believe there is no other devoted exclusively to the production and distribution of books for career missionaries and their home churches.

About the Author. James Erskine Mitchell is a native of Edgemoor, South Carolina, the son of Ethel Orr Williams Mitchell and the late George Franklin Mitchell. On graduating from Rock Hill High School he entered Erskine College, Due West, South Carolina, where he received his B. A. degree in 1961. At that time he was appointed as a missionary under the Board of the Associate Reformed Presbyterian Church to go to Mexico. He has served for one and a half terms there as administrator of the Neill Erskine Pressly Clinic. His inimitable ability to work with the nationals in many varying capacities has given him a clear insight into the problems of mission work at the present as well as a vision of the course the mission endeavor will take in the future.

On returning to the field in 1970 after a year's study in the School of World Mission and Institute of Church Growth, Fuller Theological Seminary, Pasadena, California, Mr. Mitchell will once more assume his duties as clinic administrator and will in addition take an active role in Synod's program of evangelism.

DATE DUE

NOV 5 '73			
DEC 19 197			
AR 31 '89			
MAY 8 '89			
IO 9 '92			
MY 18 93			
12/31/94			
NO 24 '99			

GAYLORD

PRINTED IN U.S.A.